Praise for "

MW00856954

"*Good financial advice, whether delivered in person or by the written word, is a skillful combination of science, art, and (mostly) people savvy. Mark Bertrang delivers each of these ingredients in just the right proportion in his delightful new book "Investments Don't Hug." If you're looking for a dry tome that discusses mutual fund expense ratios to the fourth decimal point, you can skip this book. But if you're looking for practical solutions to the financial issues faced by normal people in today's busy world, this book is for you. Mark takes us on a journey through the real life stories of families he has served through the years, teaching us lessons along the way that must not be missed. Thank you, Mark, for your contribution to the betterment of your clients' lives and to the lives of everyone who reads this excellent book!*"

—Byron R. Moore, CFP®
*Wisdom on Wealth* syndicated columnist and radio
personality
Ruston, Louisiana

"*Through my work within the Prosperity Economics Movement, extensive time is taken to calculate the value of using the economics of life insurance to enhance an individual's life today while clients are alive, enjoying their lives. Mark Bertrang reminds all of us in his book "Investments Don't Hug" that the centerpiece of this unique product is the certainty it provides families; not only for today, but the impact it has into future generations. The stories are powerful and the message is timeless.*"

—Kim D. H. Butler
Prosperity Economics Movement
Mount Enterprise, Texas

*"Life insurance planning is a very important part of a person's comprehensive financial plan. Just like a customized, comprehensive financial plan, life insurance planning should also be customized for each individual or family. Mark Bertrang explains the importance of having a focused advisor on your side with a steady hand and a knowledge base to walk through the landmines that could lay hidden to the casual observer. Mark's book shares real-life examples of what can occur in a family's life. Likewise, the explanation of how life insurance works, comparing it to how a home mortgage works, makes a complicated issue easier to grasp."*

—Frank Cherniawski, CFP®,
Wealth Management Institute
Lansing, Michigan

*"Effective estate planning requires collaboration and communication between a client's professional advisors. Throughout "Investments Don't Hug," Mark Bertrang encourages and recommends that clients work with a financial advisor, as well as with a qualified attorney and accountant. A team approach of professional advisors is important to make sure the goals and objectives of a client are being met, whether through the terms of a will or trust or through the way in which beneficiaries are designated. Bertrang illustrates the importance of this team approach through the stories he shares."*

—Gregory S. Bonney, JD
Johns, Flaherty & Collins, SC
La Crosse, Wisconsin

*"It is nice to see, in written words, the ease of understanding something complex. Mark Bertrang has done a great job in making the value of life insurance very clear and understandable. The analogies used, and real life scenarios, bring to life that it is not about the product, but about the process and people. It is the uniqueness of family dynamics, dealing with perception and misperception, that I believe this book touches on very well. We see so many families having to deal with crisis and knowing the planning that was done years before will come to fruition. This book is a must read for families. It should be a call to take action."*

—J. Grady Jennings, Executive Director
The Dignity Group
Ontario, California

*"As a software developer for the financial services industry I spend my days calculating numbers as to efficiency of one strategy over another. Life insurance can provide multiple opportunities for an individual to enhance their financial life. But, unlike a car, a refrigerator, or a stove, life insurance doesn't come with an owner's manual. Instead, after a few months and certainly a few years, the owner of life insurance may have forgotten the reasons for the original purchase and the benefits it provided in the first place. Mark Bertrang has helped to outline, through stories and easy to understand examples, how the product of life insurance works and how it has impacted forever the families that he has served."*

—Todd Langford
TruthConcepts.com
Mt. Enterprise, Texas

*"Mark Bertrang has done an extraordinary job of bringing his years of experience, clarity, and compassion to this book, "Investments Don't Hug." The joy and sorrow of each chapter builds your understanding of a potentially boring topic we often put off or never talk about—life insurance. I expected a dry formal explanation of this financial asset. Instead, I was moved by Mark's vivid examples of real-life experiences and the easy to understand explanations of how this product works and the important value it creates."*

—Adrienne Duffy
Big Futures, Inc.
Edmonton, Alberta, Canada

*"Life insurance provides the security of knowing that our loved ones will be taken care of, even if we are not around. It assures us that our hopes and dreams for them can still be accomplished. We should try to look at our dying objectively, and realize what effect it will have on the survivors. They will need time to cope and adjust, so giving them adequate financial security with life insurance is essential. Life insurance can provide immediate cash, income tax free, right when it is needed most. Mark Bertrang hasn't just communicated this, but has made this product come alive through personal stories that he has lived and now shares with the reader of the walk he has taken through the lives and deaths of his own clients."*

—Kenneth Morrison, CPA
Morrison & Associates, S.C.
La Crosse, Wisconsin

*"Here's a secret: CPAs and financial advisors are in the comfort business. Beyond the discussion of tax deductions and market risk, we provide comfort that all aspects of your financial affairs have been considered. "Investments Don't Hug" is a roadmap to give you comfort that your family is secure should you become disabled or after you die. Mark's idea of "embracing the life insurance asset" is ideal for your overall estate plan. I highly recommend this book as you make plans for you and your family."*

—Douglas H. Chaffins, CPA
Chaffins, Batdorf & Austell, LLC
Marietta, Georgia

# Investments Don't Hug

~

Embracing the Life Insurance Asset

MARK BERTRANG, CLU, ChFC

*Dedication*

For: Betty, Brianne, & Kevin

Three reasons I embrace the life insurance asset.

# Table of Contents

*Foreword*

Life insurance is a topic that's rarely on the forefront of people's minds. It reminds us of complex and unpleasant topics … financial planning, taxes, and our own mortality, to name a few. It is a product that people recognize as a need, yet are hesitant to purchase. The reasons for not purchasing life insurance are many, and those who have made the selling of life insurance their life's work hear them day-in and day-out.

So why would anyone want to be a life insurance agent? In my nearly 40 years in the life insurance industry, it is a question I have asked myself many times. Very few who embark on this career become successful. The work is hard, you face a lot of rejection, and in the early years, there are scant financial rewards. I have met many aspiring life insurance agents in my time, and I always ask them why they got into the business. Some will say they've sold various products in the past, and they thought they would give life insurance a try. Others say they've heard there's good money to be made. And there are those who talk about helping families and small businesses with their financial security. Now I've never taken a formal poll, but based on what I've seen, it's those in the last category that have the greatest chance of success.

In this book, Mark Bertrang gets into the crux of what it really means to be an exceptional life insurance agent. It isn't about the ability to explain the inherent complexities of various types of life insurance products; it isn't about preparing ledgers of numbers projected over the next 30 years or more; and it certainly isn't about making a sale and moving on to your next customer. It is about developing long-term relationships. It is about being there to help families cope, both emotionally and financially, when the unthinkable happens.

One thing that comes across clearly in this book is the passion Mark has for his life's work. The experiences he shares are both enlightening and emotional. Much of the literature about the life insurance industry focuses on the technical aspects of the business. Mark has taken a very different approach, emphasizing through his poignant stories the social good provided by life insurance benefits. A life insurance policy is a contract, a legal document between two parties. Mark illustrates that our business is about more than the paper policies are written on... it's about people's lives and the financial security that life insurance can provide.

Stephen M. Batza, FSA, MAAA, CLU, ChFC
President & CEO
Mutual Trust Life Insurance Company
*A Pan-American Life Insurance Group Stock Company*

# *Disclaimer*

How many of us while watching television have seen a commercial appear on the screen with a sports coupé speeding through the open countryside or racing through the downtown streets of a metropolitan cityscape? Because of the automobile company's legal department, small print suddenly appears at the bottom of the advertisement stating "Do Not Attempt." Isn't that silly? Do you really think you can simply jump into a flashy sports car and take to the road, as if you're a professional driver on a closed course? Certainly not; but the car company needs to protect itself from those people who aren't firing on all cylinders.

Here's the deal. When I have a plumbing problem, I call a qualified plumber. When I have an electrical issue, I call a licensed electrician. When I have my car serviced, I take it to an experienced mechanic. This should be a no brainer. "But, Mark," you might ask, "Aren't you paying more than you would if you were to just do these projects yourself? Can't you simply look it up on the internet?" Listen to me, these qualified men and women do this for a living, I don't. You should be the expert at what you do. Let these professionals be the experts at what they do. A plumbing mistake could flood my house. An electrical error could kill me! A blunder with my car could cost me the price of a new car or the safety of my life. In fact, after I finished the manuscript for this book, I hired a professional editor to help mold each chapter to communicate the information and stories I have painstakingly compiled over the past several years. I am not an editor.

Now, with that out of the way let me continue. This book is meant to give general information about the subject matter covered. I am not providing legal or tax advice within the pages of this book. If I were, the United States Congress would change the laws and tax code as soon as this book is printed anyway. Any calculations that I may discuss are for illustrative purposes only. Your situation is unique and requires the guidance of a qualified advisor—an advisor who works for you! So, use an accountant for the tax stuff and an attorney for the legal stuff.

As the author, I have approached the creation of this work with great care. However, neither I nor my publisher assume any responsibility for any errors or omissions. Also the author and publisher specifically disclaim any liability resulting from the use or application of the information contained herein. The information presented is not intended to serve as professional advice related to individual situations.

The goal of this book is to open a conversation between you and a qualified advisor or life insurance agent to achieve the specific goals outlined by your own values, for you and your family. Just like the driver navigating the closed course in our automobile commercial example, this book is to help provide an overview of the possibilities of embracing the life insurance asset. Driving the landscape of your life requires specific actions to navigate the terrain of your own financial situation.

The discussions within these pages are based upon generic policies available in the general market place. Each company and each product may contain distinctive characteristics of guarantees, non-guaranteed dividends, riders, and contract language. This requires not only a licensed life insurance agent but, in the author's opinion, an agent with qualifications showing that the person you choose to work with is a serious student of the product. Here, I am biased. A person with the designation of a Chartered Life Underwriter (CLU®) earned through The American College has shown that he or she takes this life insurance stuff very seriously. Though not a requirement, the considerable amount of work that it takes to receive a CLU® designation makes it a definite credential to consider when choosing an advisor.

Now that I've taken care of the legal disclosures, please take a moment and grab a highlighter and a pen. As you read, you should be making notes in the margins of this book while also marking those passages that specifically speak to your own situation. It is my hope that you'll enjoy reading this book, but more importantly, given the opportunity to hear the stories that have been part of my professional career, my real hope is that you will take action that could substantially change your life and that of your family for generations into the future.

Let's begin.

# Introduction

*"I'm not going to be one of your stories."*

Our embrace ended and as I looked at Jenny, her head covered by a colorful bandana, evidence of multiple chemotherapy treatments, her eyes met mine and she softly, yet sternly said, "I'm not going to be one of your stories."

An analytical financial advisor explains concepts with numbers, graphs, and charts. That never really worked for me. It felt cold, and I found it difficult to discuss a person's life using projections of hypothetical situations and numbers. Instead my decades of experience have provided me with real examples of how life actually plays out. Jenny knew that, because in my office she and her husband, Brian, had listened to many of my stories.

-----

Two rules have always been a part of my practice. Number one: privacy. Usually during my very first appointment with a new client I would say "Everything said here (at my office conference table), stays here." It was a promise that I wanted every client to understand, so they could feel free to share with me whatever was going on in their lives, without any fear that I would share their personal story with someone else. I always reminded them that this trust also went both ways, as I would often share personal stories about my own life, and I would expect the same confidentiality from them. We would be in this together.

Second, the best way I knew how to explain why any particular option should be considered for their own financial situation over another was to share a true story about a real client, though I would never share an actual name, unless I had been given permission from that person. So my stories usually centered upon the fictitious names of Robert, Rob, Bob, Roberta, or Bobbie. Whenever I used those names, it was automatically understood that I was referring to a real situation I had experienced in my practice, only the names had been changed.

-----

During the Christmas season, I enjoy volunteering for the Salvation Army ringing bells at a local grocery store. I like to sing aloud as passers-by drop their loose change into the red kettle. It's a prime spot; not outside in the cold weather and not quite inside the store, either. Instead the spot is perfectly situated in a heated corridor out of the elements, as people pass through heading toward the parking lot with shopping carts filled with overflowing brown paper bags for holiday parties. I always enjoy singing "Santa Claus is Comin' to Town" during these two-hour stints, because whether it's a senior citizen, a middle-aged housewife, little children, or greasy men running an errand on the way home from a factory shift, there's a certain magic that makes their eyes sparkle when you look at them with a smirk and sing, "So, you'd better be good, for goodness sake."

I was surprised to see Jenny coming through the automatic sliding doors on her way out of the store with her own groceries that afternoon. It had been five months since the discovery of her tumor. The doctors initially told her that they were 98 to 99 percent certain it would be benign. It wasn't. I saw Jenny during what she called her "week of freedom." She was between chemotherapy and radiation treatments. She looked great. She always did, with the most delightful smile.

I had met Jenny and Brian seven years earlier when she was only 27. They were both schoolteachers. Jenny loved teaching. But now, the cancer had put her career on hold, just as the school year began with her first class of kindergarteners.

"I'm not going to be one of your stories," she said to me after our hug. "But, you already are," I replied, "because of your determination in fighting this thing."

-----

This book contains a series of stories, each with a message of how the decision of owning the simple product of life insurance provided the promise of financial certainty for my clients and their families. Interspersed between these stories are explanations of the interworkings of life insurance in simple layman's terms. Over the decades, I don't ever remember an investment client giving me an embrace or a hug because of what an investment did for them. Investments are important. But, I have never seen an investment affect a client's life in a "life-changing" way as life insurance has.

This book is written so husbands and wives, and moms and dads, can better understand the importance of the promise of financial certainty life insurance can provide, not only after an unexpected death, but while we are living. That's something I have found investments have a hard time doing.

This book is also written for advisors to have a better understanding, that though investments can be exciting and "sexy," it is essential to understand that investments lack the certainty that can be assured not only today, but well into the future. A recent study indicated that most advisors don't want to talk about this non-investment product, because they find it too complicated to understand themselves and too complex to explain to their clients. I want them to know that "investments don't hug;" and to truly serve their clients, their friends, and their family they need to "embrace the life insurance asset." My hope is that I will make the complex story of life insurance easy to understand.

It is also my hope that investment advisors and insurance agents will use this book to reacquaint themselves with this sometimes misunderstood or simply forgotten product. This is a book that they should feel comfortable passing along to clients to help them grasp the importance of this asset and how it can work. It can be used as a primer, to begin the conversation about the security of one's family and using life insurance as a potential repository for a family's "safe" money.

Jenny's story and all the other stories contained within the chapters of this book should help to provide a blueprint to more fully understand the benefits of owning this unique product. Some people have never heard the story of how this product works. That is sad. Because advisors are missing an opportunity to be embraced for the work they do; and clients are missing an opportunity to embrace added certainty in their lives.

Over the years of my career I have lost countless clients to death. After Jenny passed, I began thinking of each one and soon realized they could tell the stories of how life insurance works better than I could. I was there at the beginning of each story, through the middle, and I was there at the close of their lives. Through each story, I learned a little more about the importance of the work I had done for each of these clients and their families.

Over the past several years, I went back and visited some of these families in their homes; some visits were in my office. I was surprised at how open many families were in sharing their stories, actually taking the time to review my notes and this manuscript for accuracy. Only a very few names have been changed, but all the stories are real. I will be forever indebted to each for the close relationships I have made throughout these years of my career.

Thank you for letting me be a part of each of your stories.

Investments Don't Hug

# Chapter One

*The best asset purchased in his short lifetime.*

"Oh, my God. Oh, my God. Oh, my God." I remember saying that softly to myself as I stared at the morning newspaper. My three-year-old daughter, sitting in her blue fabric-lined Graco® highchair was eating breakfast next to me and like a parrot, repeated the words that I had just spoke aloud. "Oh, my God."

-----

I had begun my financial career only four years earlier after leaving a job in broadcasting. Initially, I left the work as a staff announcer because of the money: the lack of it. Life was definitely simpler then. It was also much more modest. To have an increase in income would require a change of career. My wife, Betty, and I hadn't realized how little we were making, because we were focused savers and we were young and somewhat naïve, living for "today." In the beginning, it was all about us. In fact, we didn't even try having children until we had been married for about six years.

When we decided after our first full year of marriage to travel to Great Britain for a two-week fall vacation, it didn't seem difficult at all to save for a year in advance. Today, it seems like many couples simply put the expenses of trips on their credit cards. Instead, we just stopped going out to eat, and we stopped buying new clothes for the next year to put away the money we needed for the big trip. We even asked our landlord if we could dig up part of the backyard of the duplex we were renting to plant a vegetable garden. We felt rich. During that one year, we successfully saved twenty percent of our very modest annual income. I think my father-in-law, Bill, was thinking we were saving for a house. But the trip across the ocean was what we were focused on.

It wasn't until my younger sister Michelle graduated with a masters degree in speech pathology, excitingly announcing her starting pay for her first job post-college during a family gathering, that Betty and I quietly looked at one another realizing that her annual income right out of school would be thirty-five percent more than our combined incomes—Betty as a daily newspaper reporter and I as a small town radio announcer. It was a very frustrating ride home from that family get-together.

Resumes were prepared and mailed and interviews conducted. I took a position in a commissioned advertising sales job at a local radio station. The new job was located in a small college town located along the Mississippi River in the southeastern corner of Minnesota. A month later, Betty joined me after landing a position as a daily newspaper reporter in the same community. Our income increased, but so did our expenses; and new to us was the uncertainty of my "commissioned" paychecks. After a couple of years we bought a very modest home. It was only a total of six hundred and seventy-two square feet! That first house hardly equals the size of our current three-stall garage. But, it's what we could afford, at least most of the time.

The pressure of a sales job was frustrating for me and for my spouse. At one point, Betty looked at me squarely in the eyes and said, "I don't care how much you make. But, could you just make the same amount each month?" Advertising sales always experienced highs and lows; and during the lows, I became the best sales person of all. I once sold my high school alto saxophone to make a monthly mortgage payment. Another time, the monthly mortgage was paid from the sale of a moped I owned.

With time, experience and maturity, I began to settle into my new career. But, it wasn't a calling. It was a job.

After eight years in the broadcasting industry—several of which were in advertising sales—I was approached by a friend who thought I should consider a career in the financial services industry. It required licensing and additional education beyond where my original training and education had been focused. What captivated my interest more than anything else was the chance to build enduring relationships and to make a difference for the people who would become my clients. Tom's story would be an early example of the difference I wanted to make.

-----

I met Tom two years into my new career. It's not unusual to find that the majority of a financial advisor's clients are within a decade either side of their own age. There is a certain comfort level working with people who share the same life experiences and values that you do. Tom and I were only a couple of months apart in age. He worked for a local farm family as a hired hand and did some extra work on the side at a small farmers' cooperative.

I had grown up in a small rural community myself spending most summers of my early teens working for farmers weeding soybean fields, detasseling corn, and picking rocks out of fields by hand prior to the spring planting of crops. When I was sixteen, my high school classmates and I graduated from field work to work in a local vegetable canning factory, which provided a way to finance our future post secondary educations. I'm not sure if the hours we worked then as teenagers would even be legal today.

Humorously, we would joke that you could have a choice of working the shift that was either "seven o'clock-to-seven o'clock" or the shift that was "seven o'clock-to-seven o'clock;" its just that one of the shifts was "PM" and the other shift was "AM." It didn't really matter though, since every two weeks; there was a shift rotation, which in essence forced an eighteen-hour workday with a modest break in the middle to catch some sleep. Unfortunately, that's how the youth in my little town of Le Sueur, Minn., spent their summers, since the Green Giant factory often ran continually for twenty-four hours per day over the summer, only to shutdown occasionally to clean the factory.

Whether it was peas or corn, when they were ripe and ready for canning, there was no delay. When I was eighteen years old, one of my paystubs documented forty-six hours of overtime during one week. That was a total of eighty-six hours of work for that week! Even today, it's sometimes hard to shake the values of knowing that you just have to put in the hours required to get the job done. Those twelve-hour shifts paid for a lot of education for our small town's youth.

Because of scheduling conflicts, I never had the opportunity to meet Tom and his wife together. He had more flexibility with his schedule allowing me to meet with him during the day, while his spouse was at work. Plus, Tom was "old school." He was in charge of their financial decisions. Looking back, I don't recall all of the conversations that took place in that old, white farmhouse in the country. But I do remember he wanted to make sure the bills would be paid, and his wife of just two years wouldn't have to worry about money if he were to die.

Simple enough. We applied for his life insurance coverage and named his spouse as the beneficiary. Since Tom had a modest income, this would be our first step together, as he began to plan for the future.

I recall asking my manager once if I was doing enough for my clients. He reminded me that I couldn't do it all at once, that most of my clients hadn't even begun doing anything for their future, and that if I helped them move ahead with just one positive financial decision they would be far better off than if they had never met me. For the time being, I would have to be satisfied with that response.

Time moved on with more clients and more appointments. Tom and I spoke several times after I delivered his life insurance policy. But, the money wasn't quite there yet for him to take the next step to begin a savings plan. Time passed.

-----

I began that morning pretty much the same as any other morning. Betty was already up and off to work commuting north along the Mississippi River for about a half hour. We were now living in a much bigger house, located downstream in a larger river community in Wisconsin. My daughter was eating breakfast in her highchair and I was reading the morning newspaper, as the sun began to peek through the kitchen window and birds ate at a feeder near an ash tree in our backyard. That's when I saw Tom's name. There had been an accident, a snowmobile accident.

At first, I didn't read the full story, and focused only on the last name, I thought to myself, "Oh, Tom's dad died." But, it wasn't Tom's dad. It was Tom. He was only thirty-one years old, just like me. As I stared at the newspaper, I softly said to myself: "Oh, my God. Oh, my God. Oh, my God." At which, my young toddler repeated those words back to me.

I question when advisors will sometimes say that they can provide unbiased opinions. They are lying; and not only to others, but to themselves. We are all an accumulation of our life experiences. Just ask any seventy-year-old advisor, which is best: a fifteen-year mortgage or a thirty-year mortgage. The answer will always be a fifteen-year mortgage. Why? Because of age bias; the elderly advisor can't image a life thirty years into the future, when he or she will be turning one hundred years of age.

The day I looked at that newspaper, I knew subconsciously that I would now also have a bias. Tom trusted me to take care of things for him, if he couldn't. This was the moment my job really began for him and for me; it made my career a passion.

The first time I met Tom's wife was at his funeral at a small Lutheran church in a small community nearby. I don't know if she recognized me because of a photo that was on my business card, but when we met, in the back of that church, as mourners were filing in, we hugged and all I said was, "I'm so sorry. But, Tom made sure you wouldn't have to worry about the money. I'll take care of everything for you." Even though we had just met, we continued to hug and shared our tears together.

When we met a week after the funeral, I was surprised she didn't even know how much life insurance Tom owned. They had never talked about it.

This was my very first death claim on a policy I had written for a client. After sitting down with our company office manager who had several decades of experience, I felt prepared with the forms she had reviewed with me. I got into my car and traveled the twenty miles, eventually driving up the gravel driveway, to that little white farmhouse where I had last visited with Tom. This visit would be with his spouse and her parents who were there for support, as I filled out a death claim and asked for an original copy of Tom's death certificate. Unfortunately, this meeting would also include an additional form that seldom needs to be completed—an investigative form.

Usually, when a death occurs, insurance companies move rather quickly to pay a death claim. Over the years, I have found that typically a claim can be processed and paid within about ten business days after the company receives all the completed paperwork and a death certificate. In fact, most people are surprised to learn as beneficiaries that interest is even paid on the claim from the date of death until the check is processed to be delivered. But, Tom died during the "contestability period."

Life insurance companies generally have a contestability period written into their life insurance contracts. It protects the insurance company from unfairly having to pay questionable death claims. It also helps to make sure that the pricing of their products remains fair for all of their customers.  In a nutshell, the incontestability clause is similar to a "statute of limitations." This clause typically lasts for the first two years of a life insurance contract, protecting the insurance company from "martial misrepresentations" made in the original application (i.e. fraud).

After the first two years of a life policy have elapsed, the incontestability clause prevents the insurance company from denying a claim for any reason.  Tom had died only thirteen months from the issue date of his policy.  The turnaround time on his death claim wouldn't be ten business days. I actually had no idea how long the wait would be. Worse yet, I couldn't find anyone within the company that could provide me with an answer. It would all depend upon how long it would take for the company to conclude its investigation.

While I sat in the farmhouse kitchen on that winter morning with Tom's widow and her parents, we completed all the regular forms. But, we also completed the additional paperwork that required me to list all of Tom's close friends, also listing possible doctors Tom may have seen. I also had to ask many of the same questions that were on Tom's original life insurance application regarding Tom's habits, driving record, and possible drug or alcohol use. Under the circumstances, these questions were very uncomfortable for me to ask. But this process, which involved a death claim of a recently issued policy, is a standard procedure for any life insurance company. I apologized and tried to explain why the company asked me to complete the additional forms and ask such personal questions.

I remember waking up in the middle of the night thereafter, asking myself, "Did I ask all the health questions with the amount of detail I should have in Tom original application? Did I write down all of Tom's answers with as much detail as I should have? Did I make any mistakes?" It's hard not to begin second-guessing everything I did well over a year earlier. Tom trusted me then. I hoped that I hadn't made a mistake.

The investigation into Tom's death claim lasted nearly three months, which I was told later, was relatively normal. Interviews were made with Tom's close friends, past medical records were reviewed, and everything passed the test of the insurance company's claims and legal department. I finally had a check in my hands written out to Tom's wife. It was now spring. I drove out into the countryside, watching farmers coming out of their hibernation, ready to prepare for planting once the frost in the ground was gone for good. The warmth of the sun felt good as I exited my car to deliver Tom's money. Tom's widow and I talked about the frustrating and unfortunate amount of time that had passed while we waited for the claim to be finalized. We talked about Tom and we talked about what laid ahead. We hugged. This was the best asset Tom had purchased in his short lifetime.

-----

When a death claim is made on behalf of the insured, it's usually years in the future. It is highly unusual for a claim to be made early in the life of a policy. But, we don't know "the when." If we did, we wouldn't make the purchase of life insurance until perhaps a week before our death. So, since we don't know the date, it's important that an application for life insurance is one hundred percent accurate. Seldom have I ever seen anyone actually look through their life insurance policy. If they did, they might be surprised to see a copy of their original application included as part of the life insurance document. This is called the "entire contract clause." This clause protects the insurance company and the insured. It's as important as every other contract word in the policy, so it has to be perfect. Our office typically types the client's answers onto the application, so the forms can be reviewed prior to being signed. I don't want anything to be left unanswered or incomplete.

As a tool to help prospective buyers of life insurance, our office asks clients to complete an initial health and avocation form so we have an idea of the potential problems we could encounter when a client includes life insurance as part of their overall planning. I have seen college educated women with three children under the age of ten, dismissing the disclosure of having been to a clinic or hospital or of even seeing a doctor within the last decade. When asked, what about your kids? Did you give birth at home? Have you had a physical recently? I have often received replies like "Oh, I didn't think that mattered." When dealing with a contract—and that's what a life insurance policy is, a contract—everything has to be documented, no matter how insignificant it might seem.

Before an agent signs his or her name, and before a potential client signs their name, it is imperative that they pause and read what answers they have provided on an application. If the information is materially misrepresented, and typically, if death occurs before the end of the first two years of the policy, the beneficiaries could find themselves without the insurance money they thought their loved one had left for them and instead they may only receive back the premiums that were paid, plus some modest interest.

Less than two years earlier, Tom created a life insurance asset that would now continue to embrace his wife for years to come.

Investments Don't Hug

# Chapter Two

*"Could you come to the hospital?"*

It was Todd on the other end of the telephone. The doctors had told him that Nancy, his wife of almost eighteen years, would probably have another two weeks of life. Usually I don't even come into the office on Fridays because of the ten-hour days I often work during the week. In fact, I sometimes describe my work as being similar to the long back-to-back shifts of someone in the medical field: "After several days of long shifts, you really don't want me to be your nurse, if you need blood drawn. I'll be able to do it, but I may have to poke you three times to hit a vein. You would probably be happier if we do the lab work after a long weekend." But this was Nancy. She and Todd had become more to me than just clients. I would make my way to the oncology unit that morning, because of Todd's phone call.

-----

I met Nancy and Todd sixteen years earlier. They had a brand new daughter. Megan was only a month old. I could thoroughly appreciate the excitement they were experiencing as new parents. Betty and I had been married for eleven years ourselves with a three-year old-daughter at home and our new infant son.

This was a wonderful time of my career before the economics of time management forced me to have clients meet with me at my office. Our first meeting took place at their home, a little rented house on Wood Street in a blue-collar section of town where extended families would often live near one another in the same neighborhood. Todd worked for a trucking company, and Nancy was a CPA at a local accounting firm. I was invited to help them do some very basic planning because of the new addition to their lives.

There's something special about being invited into someone's home. You get to see how they live and what's important to them by examining what they might have hung on their walls or the photos of family members displayed. A visit to a family's home can also turn out to be somewhat chaotic.

Once, I was invited to visit with a couple in a rural community about an hour's drive from home early in my career. When I arrived, "Dad" was in the shower after a long day of work; "Mom" was in a rocking chair covering up a newborn she was nursing with a small blanket, and an older brother, a toddler, was playing with his toys in the corner of the kitchen. As my visit continued while waiting for "Dad" to shed the dirt from his job, all of the sudden, "Mom" had this look of horror on her face yelling for her husband – "Jack!" As I turn around to see what had happened, I saw the toddler approaching ready to hand me a "full"—and I do mean "FULL"—diaper that he had just taken off by himself, figuring I would know what do with the "gift."

That first evening with Nancy and Todd was less exciting, but the beginning of much more. We applied for life insurance for Todd, life insurance for Nancy, and we talked about a college fund for Megan. Then we did what we always did. We enjoyed one of Nancy's fabulous desserts. There was never a meeting with Nancy and Todd that didn't involve dessert at the end to finish off our visit.

As a financial advisor, it's important to surround yourself with experts in multiple disciplines. A well-connected advisor should be able to make recommendations of attorneys, accountants, bankers, mortgage lenders, realtors, plumbers, electricians, doctors, and churches. Over the years, Nancy would become my go-to person for technical tax and accounting information for clients. If an unusual situation arose for one of my clients, she was on my office telephone quick-dial for an answer to a question or to help supply the supporting documentation or reference material I would want to pass on.

In addition to our regular meetings with Todd and dessert, I would ask Nancy out for long lunches each year to express my appreciation for her assistance and her friendship. This also allowed her to share the other chapters of her life, like the time she shared the story of Todd witnessing the ultrasound when she became pregnant a second time and the doctor pointing out that they were going to have twin boys. Nancy said he just sat there in a complete state of shock, not saying a word, only looking ahead at the monitor in disbelief.

Or there was another occasion when Nancy shared that she had a cancerous melanoma removed from her back, describing the "chunk" the surgeon had taken. They believed they got it all.

Or the time, several years later, when we took a longer lunch than usual. The cancer had come back. She was being treated with chemotherapy and was wearing a wig that we both laughed about, because it was perfect, and because with her busy life, she had never had the time for perfectly styled hair before. Nancy always had a smile that looked a little bit like a smirk. You just couldn't help but smile when she was in the room. That last lunch was at least two hours long. In fact, at one point I said, "You probably should be getting back to work." She had taken a position with an engineering firm a few years earlier. "I suppose," she said. "They've been real understanding." We hugged a real long hug. It would be our last.

-----

When I arrived to Nancy's cold, colorless hospital room that Friday morning, I couldn't really be prepared. It was sixteen years since we had applied for those first life insurance policies. Megan was sixteen now and the boys— Derrick and Jeffrey—were twelve. There were just the three of us in the room: myself, Todd sitting in a chair, and Nancy in bed. I went over to Nancy who looked exhausted and I gently touched her on the shoulder. I shook Todd's hand and even with his six-foot-two and three hundred-plus pound frame, he wasn't the large man I always remembered. Nancy's illness had beaten him down, too.

I am not an attorney. But, over the years I have facilitated countless legal documents. Life insurance is a great start to a financial plan, since without money there really can't be much of a financial plan. During the first decade of my career, I strongly "suggested" to clients that they meet with an attorney to complete their wills or trusts, their financial powers of attorney, the healthcare directives, and disposition forms, as part of their overall planning.

Now, I tell clients upfront: I won't do any work for them unless these legal documents are completed or updated if need be, by a qualified attorney, as part of the process of working with me. If they say no, then it becomes a complete nonstarter for me.

My experience is that often this demand is received by "Finally, we're going to get this done," by the wife. For some reason, husbands usually are content to put these conversations off. But wives are usually the ones who "get it."

As part of our work, our office created an eight-page will fact-finder years earlier as a starter kit, to assist in the conversation with couples, not about the "what if," but for the "when." The first page of this form is usually the most difficult: "In the event of our death, where do our children go, or more specifically, to whom?" I have seen couples delay having their wills written for years because this first decision could not be made. Sometimes I would try and shock couples into a discussion by saying, "Perhaps we should just write in what county court judge you would prefer to choose the guardian for you, when you're dead."

I always ask clients once they have decided on the "who," to make a point to take the couple or individual they've chosen out for dinner and during the meal ask them if they would be willing to take care of the most important thing in their lives and to explain how important this decision is and what would really be involved if they were to say yes. Then I suggest that they do not accept an answer at that moment. But, instead allow the chosen couple to consider what they're really agreeing to over the next week or so, before asking again. I still remember when Betty and I asked her sister, Judy, and her husband, John, at a Mexican restaurant three months before our first child was to be born. We valued how they were bringing up their children and wanted our children to be surrounded by the love we knew they could provide.

But, Nancy and Todd didn't have the luxury of time. I had brought to the hospital the same will template, which I had provided them multiple times over many years. I took out a pen and placed the forms on my lap and began reading the questions, "Who would you want your kids to go to?"

Over the next half hour, Todd answered most of the questions himself, since they had obviously discussed the answers together before this day. Several times, Nancy acknowledged her agreement with a heavy breath, as she passed in and out of sleep. When I was finished, I told Todd that I would get my notes to the attorney we had agreed upon and I assured them that I had already telephoned asking if he could come to the hospital after the weekend to review and have the wills signed.

On that day, Nancy's only visitors were her immediate family and me. Nancy died at 3:40 a.m., the next morning, at the age of 43.

-----

Some people might call it a "coming to Jesus moment." I decided that day to demand that all clients have their affairs in order now. That is exactly what every advisor should demand of themselves and of their clients. It's easy to understand why anyone would prefer to put off the discussion and the execution of these documents, because it says, "I'm going to die." But, my own experience and the experience I have seen in others is the sense of knowing, after they've completed these documents, that everything is going to be okay so when they die, they can know without any question, that they are not leaving behind a mess for their family.

Investments Don't Hug

# Chapter Three

*"I never took the time to enjoy a glass of Korbel with you."*

Nancy's funeral was scheduled for the Wednesday following my hospital visit at the same Lutheran church in the next small town over where I had attended the funeral for Tom, my first client to pass away, years earlier. The wake would be held nearer their home in a small farming community. I have attended three wakes at that funeral home, all for clients.

Before Nancy was ill they had moved the family out into the country, where they could have a small plot of land and the kids could have animals. This meant showing their animals for 4-H at the county fair. They were so happy about getting out of town and into the country. After Nancy and Todd set up their new home, I was invited out for one of our regular annual reviews. The evening ended with a huge bowl of ice cream. As I said earlier, you just had to have dessert.

Before Nancy got sick, Todd had suffered his own episodes with melanoma, which included specialized treatments at Wisconsin's University Hospitals. He had pulled through those treatments, and he was as strong as ever. But losing Nancy was devastating. As a CPA, she took care of the family business of bill paying and keeping the family on-track financially. That really wasn't Todd's strong point. He was now in over his head, because these were things Nancy had always done. In fact, I got the feeling he hadn't really ever needed to write out checks for the monthly bills himself.

When the proceeds arrived from Nancy's life insurance policies, our office blocked out an entire afternoon so Todd and I could spread out all the bills on a large conference table and clean up the mess that had been created over the past several months of Nancy's life. For large death claims, most life insurance companies open an estate checking account similar to a money market account for the named beneficiary of the policy, which pays modest interest each month. These accounts allow the beneficiary to take time in making decisions regarding the death proceeds during a very emotional time, instead of receiving one large check and having to decide, "What do I do with this?"

When Todd entered my office, he had the insurance checking account along with a huge stack of bills filling his large hands. When we closed the door to the conference room, we spent the first twenty to thirty minutes talking about Nancy, how the kids were doing and when he was thinking about going back to work. Todd had been acting as a caregiver for Nancy and trying to keep their kids' lives going with some sense of normalcy. He was beginning to see how his new life without Nancy would take on a lot more focus on things that she took care of in the past.

Our discussion then turned to the money, or more specifically, the bills. Over those past months some bills had been paid late and some weren't getting paid at all. Bills were never a high priority for Todd, and with Nancy's impending death, he had no stomach for spending his days worrying about bills when he was losing his spouse and his children's mother.

So, we began with the biggest one—the mortgage. "How much do you owe?" I asked. "Not a clue," was Todd's response. "Well, let's you and I make a telephone call," I replied. And that's how the rest of the afternoon went for nearly three hours. We looked at a bill, called the creditor, and I wrote a check. Todd didn't feel comfortable writing such large numbers, as he had never needed to do so. He would double-check what I wrote on each check, sign it, and then I would leave the conference room giving the check to my assistant, who would prepare it for mailing complete with an envelope and stamp. That afternoon Todd and I paid off the mortgage, all their loans, hospital bills, and every credit card. When we were finished, there was a pile of outgoing mail and a little money leftover to set aside for the kids. This was actually the easy part. The hard part was to move ahead and complete the work started that day I had visited him and Nancy in the hospital.

Todd had a strong work ethic and contagious laughter. If you needed help, he'd be there. Changing jobs while I knew him, his career took him to a moving and storage company for quite a few years. In fact, after my wife, Betty, and I purchased a building for our office, just blocks from our home, Todd and his crew moved the office furniture from the basement space I had rented for several years. Todd occasionally enjoyed finishing big projects with a glass of Korbel® brandy. Even after the long day of moving my office, we talked about it, but he had to get home, and I had to set up the office to open for business the following Monday morning.

After cleaning up all the bills at my office, Todd was busy with filling in all the other gaps left behind by Nancy. But, there was still the estate planning work to be completed. I had forwarded all the notes from our discussions to the attorney who would be drafting the will. Unfortunately, there are several steps to this process. First, to meet with the attorney to confirm the notes provided were accurate to Todd's wishes, then reviewing a draft document, and finally, the actual signing of the will. Sounds easy enough. Not so. I felt the pressure was on me. In fact, there were times that it almost seemed as if I heard Nancy's voice, "Get on him, Mark."

There were times I would contact the attorney and ask, "Has Todd been in yet? No? Then call him," I would say with an exasperated tone. I also called Todd occasionally, "Have you gone down to see the attorney yet?" I remember saying to my assistant at least once, "I think I'm going to piss off Todd soon with all my phone calls and handwritten notes to get this will completed." Thank God, he never did loose his cool over my insistence. He finally wrapped up all the loose ends. It was finished.

-----

# Chapter Three

"Shit, Todd's cancer came back," I said to myself. Everyone was concerned. I even received a telephone call at home one evening from a mutual friend who knew Todd from his childhood. "I know you can't tell me anything, Mark, but is the family going to be alright?" "Yea," I said, "Todd and Nancy have done everything they could. The family is going to be okay."

There comes a point, where it's no use to continue on with treatment. Instead, you begin to live with the inevitable outcome. Todd was placed in a nursing facility. I decided one morning to just drop by and hope it would be a good time to visit.

There are three things I remember from that day. First, even though he was tired, Todd was still playing host. We laughed and joked. Todd still complained about how heavy the reception desk from my office was to move and how he had actually wished he could have taken a chainsaw to it, instead of moving it on that day.

The second thing is that at the end of our lives, our decisions aren't ours any longer. While I was with Todd, two petite young nurses came into his room. I mention their size, because until he became ill, Todd was a big man. I asked Todd if he wished to have me leave the room, while he spoke with these nurses. He said, "No, just stay here." Earlier, Todd had asked the staff if he could leave the facility for a day, to do some small projects at home. But, these two petite nurses were there to tell big Todd that wouldn't work. The staff was fearful he might fall and hurt himself, had he left. Todd and I realized at that moment, his decisions were no longer his to make.

And third, I had a chance to visit with Colleen, Todd's sister, and her husband, Joel, as I was leaving Todd's room after a strong handshake and a goodbye. I had met Colleen and Joel before, but our connection would become important in the near future.

On my way out of Todd's room, I turned back and said, "I'm sorry; I never took the time to enjoy a glass of Korbel® with you." "Me too," he quietly replied.

Todd died days later at the age of forty-four. His daughter, Megan, was eighteen. His sons, Derrick and Jeffrey, were fourteen.

-----

Perhaps the lesson learned here is more for me than it is for you, the reader. It would have been easier not to pursue Todd repeatedly to complete his will. I learned later that his sister Colleen had also been working on him to finish this important document. I could have easily said to myself, this isn't my responsibility. This isn't my job. But a good advisor and a friend will continue to try to do what's right, even at the risk of being criticized. I continued to try and make certain Todd and Nancy's wishes would be honored. As I embraced their daughter and shook the hands of the young men their sons were becoming shortly thereafter at Todd's wake, I wanted the words "I'm sorry" to be about their loss and not about my failings to see their parents' planning all the way through.

# Chapter Four

*"How do you thank someone for raising your children?"*

What were the odds that during my career I would see both parents, clients of mine, die and leave minor children behind? I pray that my lifetime quota has been filled. Even though I tried to make sure Todd and Nancy were prepared for what I thought was a virtual impossibility, I couldn't help but question my own abilities. Had I done everything possible? They came to me to guide their planning. So, I felt responsible for whatever the outcome would be.

Looking through their files after Todd's death I began taking an inventory of everything I thought had been completed. But was it? Really? Thankfully, Todd's will was executed. At least there was a game plan in place designating what he wanted for the kids' care and their future.

As I suggest to all of my clients when making the election of potential guardians, Todd had invited his sister, Colleen, and her husband, Joel, out to his house. He said that he needed to ask them something. Colleen wasn't sure why they needed to get together. Joel said, "He's going to ask us to be the guardians for the kids." "No, he isn't," was Colleen's response. "Oh yeah," replied Joel, "that's why we're going out to the house. He's going to ask us. But, I just don't see how we can do it." Colleen responded, "Well, don't worry; I'm sure it's not that."

Yet, that was exactly the reason Todd had asked them to the house that evening. Without a moment to pause, after Todd finished asking Colleen and Joel if they would act as guardians, Joel answered, "Sure, we will." Todd continued saying that he only needed guardians to be named to complete his will and not to worry, because "he wasn't going to die."

Colleen and Joel's own children were 23 and 24 at the time of Todd's death. They were already out of the house. In fact, one of the kids' rooms had already become a guest room. It now would become the twins' bedroom.

"The addition of three children in your home changes the dynamics of your own family and your own life," Colleen told me, "especially since we had already become empty nesters." Colleen's focus now needed to be on Todd and Nancy's children.

Colleen realized that her own children would now be taking a backburner in her life. She shared with me that "suddenly my own children felt like they no longer had a family." Because Colleen and Joel's children were grown, it might have felt that way to them—that they had written them off—but they hadn't been.

"I have to deal with this right now," Colleen would say to her kids. "I'm here for you, but Todd's kids have been through hell and I have to be there for them, right now."

A sense of awkwardness continued, at times. When Colleen and Joel's own children came home to visit there wasn't a place for them to stay. Home didn't quite feel like home any longer for them.

As part of my job, I have read a lot of wills over the years and I've learned to quickly recognize those documents that appear to have been created through standard boilerplate computer programs. Remember, I am not an attorney, but I believe a document as important as the final statement of the directions for your loved ones to follow should be a masterpiece of love and caring, not an effort completed through "fill-in-the-blank" software.

When Colleen and I sat down together for the first time at my office, after Todd's death, we each had a copy of Todd's will in our hands, reading it aloud together. We came to a section of the document where it stipulated a gift to be given annually to Colleen and Joel for acting as guardians for Todd and Nancy's children. The gift, according to the will, could not be used for the kids; it was specifically for the guardians. Colleen questioned me, "What is this? Where did that come from?" I raised my hand and said, "That's because of me."

-----

I have had many conversations with married couples preparing them for the important estate planning meeting they need to have with a qualified attorney and I have always asked them, "Do you ever get away from your kids for a weekend or for a vacation, or to just give yourself a break, to keep your sanity or perhaps to keep your marriage going, or to just to be able to reconnect with one another, as a couple?" That's the idea behind the annual gift for the guardians. "Think of it as 'respite care'," I said. "If you would do this for yourself, then why wouldn't you provide the same opportunity for the guardians who will be taking care of your children?"

When Colleen and I visited together a year later, I could tell that the little light had gone on in her head and she now understood the reason for what I like to refer to as the "Guardian Thank You" clause. During that previous year, Colleen and Joel had the opportunity to visit their daughter in Denver. The trip was paid for in part as a thank you gift from Todd and Nancy, stated in Todd's will, for taking care of their children.

The planning I had recommended for Todd and Nancy wasn't as perfect as I would have liked. Wisdom comes through experience, and unfortunately, I had never had the experience of a father and mother both dying and leaving children behind. I could certainly fault the attorney, for whom this is standard work, but I blame myself as well, because it just never crossed my mind.

When the "Guardian Thank You" clause was set up in Todd's will, it allowed for a gift to be given to the guardians annually in thanks for the love and care provided to his and Nancy's children until the youngest child would reached the age of eighteen. That was the mistake.

Why?

Because it made the assumption the responsibility for caring for their kids would end after the year the twins would reach the age of eighteen, which was the year they would graduate from high school. How many parents wish their kids would actually move out of the house at the age of eighteen? How many actually do? Then, why would we expect these same children to leave the home of those who had acted as their guardians at that age?

-----

As a parent myself, I now realize how goofy that reasoning was. So, it didn't surprise me to learn that the boys weren't living on their own after high school. What kid is? If I could go back and make a different recommendation, I would have suggested the "Guardian Thank You" clause continuing until the age of twenty-one or until the adult child has actually moved from the home of those who acted as guardians while they were minors, whichever came first.

At least, I had the opportunity to help assure that there was some kind of thank you provided in Todd's will. I have seldom seen a clause of this kind ever added to a will; and I have read a lot of wills over my career. Is there a clause like this in your will? If you have children, there should be.

Remember, after Todd's death, his daughter, Megan, lived immediately with Colleen and Joel when she was eighteen years old and then into the next year. Just because she was eighteen at the time of her father's death, did that mean she was ready to go and find a place to live on her own? I don't think so. How cruel would that have been?

What's a reasonable amount to consider for an annual "Guardian Thank You" gift? Let's consider what you're asking the guardian to do: to care for, love, and nurture your children, as if they were their own. What's the value of that? I believe it's the most important job that you can bestow upon someone in your will. If you've created a trust to hold assets for your children's future, it wouldn't be unusual for a professional trustee to have an annual administration fee of perhaps one percent or more. That's an amount I would personally use as a starting point in determining the annual "Guardian Thank You" gift. Consider having at least one percent of the trust assets paid out each year to the guardians you've chosen, as a thank you. Aren't your kids worth at least that minimal amount?

If your chosen guardians need to step in to fulfill the duties of surrogate parents for you, give them the opportunity to consider taking a trip and giving themselves some respite care away from your children. Again, it should be noted that this gift money is not to be used for your children. Instead it's there for the guardians. At first, guardians may feel guilty for receiving this gift money. That's normal, as was the case for Colleen and Joel. But, remember it's a thank you for taking on an enormous job and the responsibility of raising your children. Isn't that at least as worthy as what someone may receive for payment when managing the money left inside of a trust for your children's future?

-----

Let's also discuss Social Security benefits for the minor children of the deceased. Upon the death of a parent, monthly benefit payments may begin for the benefit of the minor child. This is not a stream of money to be deposited for their future, though some of it may be used for that purpose. This money is really to be used for the here and now. It's for your children's share of the groceries, medical costs, gas to take them places; it's their share of the heat, sewer, water, electricity, and internet; and yes, if they have cell phones, it should pay for that, too. The list can go on and on.

I believe it is a disservice for the guardian to neglect itemizing the cost of caring for a minor child and to not properly seek reimbursement from the minor's monthly Social Security payments or the trust account created through the consolidation of life insurance proceeds and other assets. Unfortunately, many guardians will feel a sense of guilt, believing it is their responsibility to pay for these additional costs out of their own pocket. It shouldn't be.

Isn't this why we have life insurance and isn't this why Social Security benefits are provided for the raising of minors after their parent's death? This is why the deceased (hopefully) established a testamentary trust through their will. I have often heard guardians worry that others will think less of them because they're keeping track of these added costs for reimbursement due to raising the children of their loved ones. In Colleen and Joel's case, Joel took a job with less pay, but that would allow him to be home at night, because he felt it was the right thing to do. This was a sacrifice they were willing to take as a couple, because of the love for Todd and Nancy's children and because that's what families do.

Remember, a guardian is being asked to care for your child. It's your responsibility to provide the money, just as you would have taken that responsibility had you lived. It wasn't someone else's responsibility then. It shouldn't be now.

I believe special attention should be given regarding the stipulations about education funding instructions, as well, in your will. My wife, Betty, who has taught classes at a local university, has shared stories of students who would drop classes when their grades were going south, but because it was too late in the quarter, they (usually the parents) were out the entire cost of the class that had been dropped.

Instead of being overly generic regarding education (i.e. money can be used towards postsecondary schooling) some clients, also remembering how they partied during their school years, have suggested a "carrot and stick" approach, indicating in their will a stipulation that their child would be reimbursed after a semester of school based on their performance, such as a 100 percent trust reimbursement based on a 4.0 grade point average, 90 percent reimbursement for a 3.0 grade point average, 80 percent reimbursement for a 2.0 grade point average and no reimbursement for anything less. This could provide an incentive for the young student to become more disciplined while attending school. Not everyone would agree with this concept, and surely it isn't right for every circumstance. But what's wonderful is that you can create living directions for what's appropriate for your children and your values and beliefs.

When Betty and I completed our first will, our first child had yet to be born; we placed a stipulation that any remaining proceeds would be given to our children in the following manner: One third of their share at the age of twenty-three. Half of each child's remaining share at the age of twenty-six; and lastly, the remaining share left for each child at the age of twenty-nine. By the time Betty and I redid our will in our late thirties, I remember thinking to myself, "What were thinking back then? That's way too young to receive substantial sums of money!" Our own "new and improved older" (sic) ages provided a different prospective.

The next edition of our will broke down the remaining proceeds in the event of our death in this manner: One quarter of each child's share at the age of twenty-five; one third of the remainder at the age of thirty; one half of the remainder at the age of thirty-five and finally, each of their remaining shares would have been paid out at the age of forty. Since we were nearing the age of forty ourselves at that time, it became easier for us to wrap our minds around how our own maturity level had grown over our lifetimes and how the age of forty just didn't seem that old.

When our third will was completed, we updated this section, yet again. In our most recent edition, we have become even more specific. Since our children at the time of this writing are in their twenties, we better understand what would be appropriate for each of them at this point in their lives.

The timing and the amounts in which your money may be passed to your children do not have to be equal. There is no rule that dictates that. What you do want to accomplish is to be fair and appropriate for each child's situation.

Reading the previous section, you might be thinking to yourself—Mark, you've had three different wills!?!

Yes, that's about one for each decade of our marriage thus far. You simply shouldn't expect to have the attitude of "one and done." Life changes, your children's situations change, your financial situation changes. Think about it. How often have you gotten a new car? Exactly! Probably every ten years; maybe more often than that. Times change, needs change, and what was appropriate a decade ago may not be appropriate today. The price of a new will is probably a little less than the price of one car payment. Is your family worth that?

Let me continue with another analogy. In our home, we have a drawer where we keep the instruction manuals of each new appliance we've purchased through the years. Nowadays, you're lucky if a major appliance lasts a decade before you buy a new one. When the new one arrives at the house and the old one is taken away, we throw away the old manual and keep the new one. Doesn't your final financial plan deserve the same attention and consideration as a refrigerator or washer and dryer? A will is the instruction manual that you leave behind for your family. It needs to be up to date.

Here's something else to consider. If there is a substantial amount of money left from your estate, wouldn't it be appropriate to require the beneficiary who will receive those funds to perhaps complete a financial class, to be determined by the trustee, prior to the distribution of those assets, to teach them how to better manage those assets themselves? Maybe that should be an option for a parent to consider adding into the requirements your child has to fulfill, when creating your will.

-----

As Colleen and I continued our visit, we both agreed that everyone wants their children to have a better life than they had, but we also agreed that we don't want to just give them that life. Instead, we want to give them the tools and means to create that life for themselves. We would like to provide a safety net, not a hammock.

It's important to complete all of your estate planning documents. In Todd's will there was a section indicating that a list of personal articles would be listed separately indicating specific items be given to specific individuals. Colleen worked desperately to locate that list, only to eventually find it, incomplete. We can only guess what Todd wanted included in that document.

There are several jobs outlined in a will. Please be mindful as to not overburden those stepping in to fill your shoes. The guardian, the executor, and the trustee should be separate individuals.

In the most simplistic definitions, here is what each of these jobs entails:

- The guardian is responsible for the care of the children.

- The executor is responsible for the settling of the estate.
- The trustee is responsible for managing the money, after the estate is settled.

Colleen knew she had been named as the guardian for Todd and Nancy's children, because Todd had already asked her. What she didn't know was that she had also been named as the executor of his estate. Perhaps Colleen was the only person Todd felt comfortable doing this job. But this places a huge stress on the person serving in the capacity of both of these functions.

Fortunately, Todd had chosen a trust company to manage the estate proceeds upon his death, which was my recommendation.

Not only did Colleen have the responsibility for the care of her niece and nephews, but she suddenly had the responsibility of selling the house, property, and personal possessions, and paying all the outstanding loans, credit cards, and bills. Just like asking permission to name a guardian, I believe it's important to ask for the person's consent before naming an executor. After completing the task of closing your estate, the person you've named will know more about you than you ever wanted them to know. They have to go through every little piece of paper you have to close the financial books of your life, which includes your very last tax return.

Let me pause here and make a very strong recommendation that you never, ever, name a guardian and then also name that person to be a trustee of your financial assets upon your death. A guardian's job is to provide love and care. A trustee's job is to manage and distribute money.

Fortunately, Todd separated these two jobs. Had he combined them, it would have added one additional level of complexity to Colleen's life. Instead, when the children had questions or disagreements on how the trust was set up (per Todd's instructions in his will) or when and how they would receive money, Colleen could honestly say, "I'm sorry, honey. I'm not in charge of that."

Is your will in place? If not, then call your advisor, a friend, or a co-worker. Ask them for the name of a qualified attorney and make the appointment today; and remember a will dictates what happens after your death. Unfortunately, that requires money and the quickest, surest asset that provides those resources at exactly the moment they're needed is life insurance.

Investments Don't Hug

# Chapter Five

*Human Life Value*

Whether term life or permanent life insurance is chosen as the product to insure your life, the first question to ask is how much life insurance should you purchase? Why is it that all other forms of insurance protection are purchased based on a potential loss replacement calculation? In the event of the loss of your home due to fire or your automobile due to an accident, your goal should be to replace 100 percent of the value lost. Yet, when it comes to life insurance, the amount purchased is often based on some general theory or rule of thumb such as seven to ten times your annual income. If either of those numbers were to be used that means your insurance coverage could vary by as much as forty percent! If your house burned to the ground tonight, would you want your insurance coverage off by as much as forty percent or possibly more?

Even though an automobile is a depreciating asset, the insurance company still calculates its replacement value each year, in the event of its total loss from an accident. If you think of your life as a car, the replacement value in the event of a total loss would be death. By comparison, partial damage to a car could be analogous to a partial or total disability, not ending in death. That too, you would want to have insured. Unprepared for death, a family's life may be devastated, but in the event of a disability, you're still around to see how devastating life can become when the money that was there, i.e. your income, has now vanished.

The insurance company that insures your home performs a calculation each year to determine the replacement value of your house. This estimate is based on an annual builder's replacement value index to rebuild your house using similar materials and workmanship. That's why your homeowner's premium might automatically rise each year. The increase wasn't necessarily because of the risk of having a claim filed, but because the replacement value (or cost to replace your home) has increased simply due to inflation. So, even without making any improvements to your house during the previous year, it's still worth more, and it will take more money to replace that asset in the event of a claim.

If it existed, the best programmed life insurance policy should increase each time your income increases, because you're now worth more! Your bank knows this. As your income increases your lender would allow you to buy a bigger house and a nicer car, because they've based your potential loan repayment amounts on the value of your expected annual earnings into the future. They understand that you have a higher value to them simply by your increased earning potential.

If your car is totaled in an accident, don't you want to receive the full replacement value from the insurance company to replace it? Likewise, if your home burns to the ground in the middle of the night, leaving your family and you on the street watching the local fire department putting out the flames, upon realizing that you've lost your home and all of its belongings, don't you want it back? Don't you want it all back—the full replacement value?

-----

Over the years, my wife, Betty, and I have made many improvements to our most recent home, which is situated in a modest older neighborhood. Its location allowed our children to walk to nearby neighborhood schools when they were young. We chose the location, in part, for that reason. It also provided our family with a substantially larger lot, with large established trees, compared to those typically found in newer tightly arranged neighborhoods. Unfortunately for us, financially, the modest location doesn't enhance the resale value of our home.

Built more than forty years ago, our home was constructed with higher than average caliber building materials. In addition, we've made our own improvements over time and it has been important for us to stick with above average enhancements. We would regularly remind ourselves that the improvements we made to our home were for our enjoyment and that the probability of actually increasing the sales value of our home would be modest.

When a homeowner acquires coverage to insure their property, I am often struck that the value placed on their home's insurance replacement coverage is sometimes exactly the same dollar amount as the purchase price of their home; and yet these two values often have nothing to do with one another. After a basement remodeling project for our own home, I was finally able to convince our homeowner's insurance agent to come to our home and make a proper replacement valuation for insurance purposes. He would tell me by telephone that the amount of insurance coverage "seemed right." But, as we walked through the finished basement project together he looked up and counted ceiling lights, while shaking his head back and forth. "Is there a problem?" I asked. "Can lights," he said. "Those are expensive to replace."

We continued walking through our home for the next hour, while he made notations on his clipboard, pointing out features he didn't realize our home possessed, like the redwood siding that was hidden under a coat of white paint on our two-story colonial. He continued to make notes of hardwood, ceramic tile floors, and other unique improvements we have made over the years. The agent returned to his office and called later the next day with the replacement number I requested to properly insure our home. He was more surprised at the final number than I was.

My wife, Betty, is a realtor. So she knows real estate prices. In addition, we also had an appraisal performed on our property a year earlier, so we knew the fair market value of our home, which was confirmed yet again on the real estate tax bill from the city the previous year. My wife, the appraiser, and the city were all within ten thousand dollars of each other as to the fair market value of our home, which in theory, is the amount for which we should be able to sell our house. So, I was fairly confident as to the potential sales value of our home.

But, I knew the replacement value would be an entirely different number. In fact, the replacement value number determined by my agent's nationally respected insurance company was eighty percent higher than its fair market value. And that didn't include our "stuff"—all the possessions inside our house. It only represented the value of the quality of our home's structure. Now, let's pose this question. How much do you believe we should insure our home for: the full fair market value we would receive if we were to sell our home; or the full *replacement* value, to rebuild if our home were destroyed due to a tornado or a fire? Which home do you think my family wants to return to—the fair market value home or the home that has been restored to its full replacement value?

Guess what the insured value was prior to our insurance inspection? The same as the fair market value. Guess what we changed it to? You're right, the full, true, *replacement* value! Yes, my premium increased. But I want the full replacement value of my home insured. In the event of a claim, I want the home I had, not a lesser house.

-----

Would it be any different to replace a father or a mother? Why would anyone use a "rule of thumb" to determine the replacement value of a life? The determination of a life's value should be calculated using something more detailed than just an annual income multiplied by some assumed number, which has often been recommended by many advisors. Unfortunately, the "assumed" number can be substantially different from one advisor to the next. So, who is correct?

What if I'm more valuable than my house? I believe I am. I believe you are too. Consider that it took my property/casualty insurance agent spending more than an hour walking through my house with a clipboard, and then returning to his office to continue his calculations, to determine my home's value. Then how much more time should be spent in calculating my replacement life value or your replacement life value?

In 1927, the American College created the CLU® (The Chartered Life Underwriter) designation, which is considered to be the world's most respected designation of life insurance expertise. Upon successful completion of its program and experience guidelines, the recipient is awarded a certificate that reads in part "insuring the Human Life Value." *Human Life Value* represents the maximum amount of coverage for which an individual should be able to apply to an insurance company when considering the purchase of a life insurance policy.

When you choose automobile insurance coverage, except for the liability limits which may be required by your state of residence, the value of insuring your automobile, unless there is a loan against it, can be determined by you, and up to the maximum allowed by the insurance company. The least amount of coverage available that you can purchase is zero, because you are not required to purchase this coverage to insure the actual value of your car at all.

On the other hand, the most coverage you would be allowed to purchase to insure your automobile would be that amount determined by the automobile insurance company. You are not allowed to buy more coverage than the replacement value. As the policy owner, you cannot over-insure your automobile. You can't purchase more insurance than what your car is actually worth.

When choosing homeowner's insurance coverage, unless there is a loan again it, the lowest amount can be determined by you, the policy owner. The least amount would be zero, meaning that you've declined coverage for your house altogether. There's no one who can force you to buy insurance other than an amount you may be required to buy by your bank to protect their interest in the mortgaged amount of your home. It's not surprising that most, if not all, homeowners want and purchsase the full replacement coverage for their home, up to the maximum allowed by the insurance company. Again, you cannot purchase more coverage than your home's full replacement value. If your insurance policy were to allow more than the amount to cover a potential loss to slip through, then once a loss is filed, the insurance company won't pay you extra money after having the repairs completed. Insurance companies won't pay you a bonus if there's money left over, realizing you had coverage they never intended you to have in the first place.

This concept is called "insuring against loss." You can only purchase insurance coverage up to the loss you might sustain. You can not over insure your car, your home, or your life. Some people are misinformed by believing that an unlimited amount of life insurance coverage can be purchased. As with other potential losses, precise calculations are used to determine the potential maximum loss in the event of a death. If the agent you're working with uses the phrase "general rule" in determining the amount of insurance coverage you should have, move on to another agent. This agent doesn't know what they're talking about.

Over the years, I have been somewhat startled and amazed, as I have spoken to insurance and association groups, by how many representatives and agents do not even know the basic financial underwriting guidelines of the very companies they represent, in determining the maximum amount of life insurance coverage an individual may be allowed to apply for. Instead, most have settled on some "rule of thumb" which they may have picked up at an insurance sales seminar.

When you are trying to determine the proper amount of life insurance coverage you should have, there are several numbers you need to know. The first number is zero. Just like automobile or homeowners insurance, other than the required minimums which may be set by your state or by your lender to cover a loan, you can decide not to purchase any life insurance coverage whatsoever. No minimum requirements exist for life insurance. If zero is the number you want, stop reading right here. The rest of this book will be of no value to you; thank you for your time.

On the other hand, assuming you are moving forward with the intention of maximizing your family's future with life insurance, the next step is to determine your Human Life Value. What is your full replacement value? That would be the maximum amount of life insurance coverage you would be allowed to apply for from a life insurance company.

"So, Mark, as a 'general rule of thumb,' what would that number be?"

You must have skipped over that previous part. Please go back and reread it. There is no way that number can be calculated here. A qualified property and casualty insurance agent came to my home to calculate its replacement value and it took more than an hour of his time. Calculating your human life value also is a unique calculation to you and you alone. But, once you have that number from a qualified advisor or agent, you can move onto the next step.

So, now you have two important numbers: zero, which means no coverage is purchased, and your Human Life Value number, the maximum amount of life insurance you are able to apply for.

There is also a possible third option that should be discussed, which may allow you to exceed the usual maximum amount of life insurance coverage.

Here's an example of this unique situation. When our children were at home during the early years of our marriage, Betty and I made the decision that we wanted a parent to be at home. But, we also wanted to build our assets by making several real estate acquisitions. While at home with the kids, Betty was in charge of acquiring and managing our real estate properties, which consisted of several duplexes and a commercial office building. She also worked as the general contractor during the initial remodeling effort, which lasted nearly a half-year on the office building project.

During that time she did not have a regular job that would have shown any reportable W-2 earned income. So, regular financial guidelines greatly misstated her human life "replacement" value for our family in the event of her death. This was during a time when the debt we had taken on was substantially increased due to our real estate loans.

Betty's value was greatly underestimated in the eyes of the insurance company. So, to assist in determining her true Human Life Value, we documented the "non-wage" value she brought to our real estate investment portfolio and mathematically estimated the potential risk of loss, due to an unexpected death. the additional documentation we provided allowed us to acquire nearly three times the coverage we would be been able to apply for using the standard financial underwriting guidelines. As you can see, a simple "rule of thumb" or formula doesn't work in making these calculations.

Likewise, in my practice, I have documented the future potential earning power of some young executives and doctors who were still early in their careers for insurance companies, so we could insure the future incomes that they would be earning in upcoming years, by obtaining the coverage now, when they were young and probably still in the best health of their lives.

Often times, people wait until their health lessens before realizing the need for life insurance. You may pay a life insurance premium with money, but you actually buy it with your health. It's unfortunate, but waiting to insure your life later may have its own cost—the cost of paying more, or even being denied coverage altogether, because of your poor health.

# Chapter Six

*"We thought we were invincible."*

"I was busy preparing for a double baby shower for my cousins on that Friday in November," Mary told me. "Jim was getting ready to officiate a junior varsity basketball game at a local Catholic high school."

As he started out the door, Mary called out, "Get back here and give me a kiss." Jim returned and gave her a little kiss, at which Mary said, "I know you can do better than that!" So, he paused and gave his wife a long passionate kiss, just before leaving through the front door of the little white house where they had started their lives together just a few years earlier.

A little later, Mary would be getting their two young children, four-year-old Tommy and three-year-old Rosemary, into their snowsuits to leave on that chilly evening. Before departing, Mary found herself unexpectedly fidgeting, touching and readjusting small items around the room for no apparent reason that she could explain, except for the extra time it provided before she placed her hand on the door to leave the house. It was just at that moment the phone rang. The voice on the other end belonged to the wife of Jim's officiating partner, Mike. "Mary," she said, "something's happened to Jim. He collapsed and he's on the way to the hospital".

-----

Mary and Jim had known each other many years before they were married. At first, she was actually dating Jim's best friend. While dating, Jim told his friend, "You'd better marry that gal or I'm going to." Later, that friend would become Jim's best man.

Though you wouldn't have found Jim in church on a regular basis, Mary thought of Jim as a godly man. He never swore, he was good to everyone, but he also had a devilish grin that made her smile. After they married, Jim continued to be the affectionate and romantic man she fell in love with. But, she also realized that she wasn't the ultimate "No. 1" in his life.

Jim was the oldest of three boys, and his folks would always remain his first priority. Being an outdoorsman would be number two, because of his lifelong passion for hunting and fishing.

Rounding out the top three passions in his life would be Mary and the kids; and she was okay with that. Mary understood the happiness that all these passions brought to his life. "We were the couple that others were envious of, because we were so crazy about one another. That's just the way we were." Mary continued with a grin, "My friends would say 'I'm so jealous' and I would answer back 'you should be'."

Here's an example of how Jim showed his devotion.

"I came home one day," Mary shared, "remembering that I had told Jim I wanted a white picket fence around my garden. It was just a little garden along a pathway. When I arrived home, Jim was covered with paint from head to toe. Now, you have to understand, Jim didn't do that kind of stuff. I expected him to go out and purchase a white picket fence. But, instead he had taken little pickets and cut them down to size and made a fence for me. The paint was all over the sidewalk and it was all over him too! It wasn't even white, like our house."

Instead, he had found some cream-colored paint in their garage, so it didn't even match the house, but instead, it looked dingy and dirty. That didn't dim his enthusiasm. With a big smile on his face, he declared, "Look what I made for you!" Looking back with memories of joy, Mary says, "It was the most wonderful fence I had ever seen in my entire life!"

It came straight from Jim's heart. Mary never let him know that she had to reset the nails halfway through the gardening season, because the nails he used were too small causing the fence to begin falling apart. He didn't have any carpentry skills. But, he had made this simple "Charlie Brown" picket fence for Mary. Even Jim's mother commented to Mary, "Jim made that for you? He really does love you!"

For extra money and for the love of sports, Jim enjoyed refereeing high school basketball games. Mary nodded with a quiet joy, as she recalled how he looked in the black and white striped shirt of his uniform and matching dark slacks running from one end of the basketball court to the other, following the young players. "He had a fantastic body, let me tell you," Mary smirked, "he didn't have a piece of fat on him. He had a six-pack and he was strong."

-----

I met Jim and Mary after they had been married for just a couple of years. Jim was working at a foundry, work that he would do for a total of seventeen years. Their son, Tommy, was a toddler, and Rosemary was an infant. Mary was doing daycare in their home for added income. At this point in a couple's life, with the responsibility of a family, the debt of a mortgage, and other ongoing expenses, "saving for the future" often needs to take a backseat to having to plan for "protection," now.

We discussed their responsibilities, and they decided to add a substantial amount of additional life insurance on Jim, due to his role as the main provider for the family. Our two meetings were straight-forward. There was a definite need, and it could be covered by using life insurance. During our two separate visits, we applied for the coverage, received approval from the insurance company and put the policy into effect. Later, we planned on tackling saving for the future.

The plan we had established together sailed along smoothly, until about two years later, when I received a telephone call from Jim. He wanted to cancel his life insurance, because of a new job he was taking on. In fact, it was a brand new career. Jim had applied for and received a position with the United States Postal Service, just one community over from where they lived. Instead of being trapped indoors everyday, this would be a walking route allowing him to be outdoors, delivering mail as a neighbor carrier, with a large leather satchel hanging over his shoulder. What could be better for an outdoorsman but to be outdoors? He was thrilled with this opportunity.

In addition to being outside during his workday and having the security of employment through a governmental agency, Jim would also acquire a pension, a 401(k), a great health benefit program, and the potential for substantial amounts of life insurance coverage. Some of the life insurance was at no cost, some he would be able to purchase over time at very low group rates. The income and fringe benefits were an answer for many of his and Mary's future goals for their family.

-----

Periodically, I have come across situations like this, when a client has the opportunity to acquire life insurance coverage through an employer. These can be very important employee benefits. When there's an opportunity to take advantage of a benefit such as this, more times than not, I'll suggest doing so. But, here's the key. These are "fringe" benefits. That means they are "outside the main." It's often forgotten that these benefits are at the discretion of the employer or are renegotiated by the employee's union at the end of each contract period. The employee doesn't own the right for these benefits to continue into the future.

These benefits are at the sheer discretion of others, not you.

In fact, at normal retirement ages, most fringe benefits, such as life insurance are terminated completely, or in extremely limited cases, they might be continued at a greatly reduced benefit level. Even then, they are usually reduced to a smaller amount over the first several years of retirement, until in most cases the eventual death benefit is substantially less than what would be needed for even a basic burial.

When you purchase a life insurance policy in the open marketplace, you can choose to be the "owner" of the life insurance contact. But, when you have life insurance through an employer, a union, or an association, you become a certificate "holder." The employer, union, or association is the owner of the master contract with all the rights to keep, renegotiate, or terminate the contact. Remember, this is coverage on the "fringe." It should never be at the core of your overall planning. In addition, the master contract holder often may determine the eligibility of fringe benefits. Some of these benefits may be determined based on longevity of employment; restated another way–have you worked long enough at your current job to actually acquire the benefits your employer may offer?

In addition to having the risk of sometimes unknown life insurance coverage amounts, when the main breadwinner dies, as Jim did, the family may also lose their health insurance coverage. In Jim and Mary's case, Mary didn't have any health insurance of her own, as a daycare provider. The family also lost all of Jim's future earnings, his future pension contributions, his future 401(k) contributions, his future 401(k) contribution matches, and any additional spouse and dependant life insurance protection into the future. The fringe benefits were no longer fringe. They were now gone. The future part of Jim's future plans ended when Jim died.

When you purchase personally owned life insurance, the policy stipulations are set forth in the language of the contract. In its most simplistic form the only person who can change the policy after it's been issued is you, the policy owner.

-----

On the day Mary received that startling telephone call, the drive from Mary and Jim's house to the hospital emergency room would have taken about twelve minutes. She doesn't remember the drive at all from that day. What Mary remembers is repeating aloud again and again and again: "Oh, my God. Oh, my God. Oh, my God."

It should have taken only six short minutes from the gymnasium floor, where Jim had collapsed during the first few minutes of that winter basketball game, to arrive to the sterile regional hospital emergency room. Though the distance Mary was traveling was twice that which would bring Jim to the hospital, she arrived before the ambulance.

"I don't remember arriving at the hospital," Mary said. "I just remember standing there, asking if he was there yet; and he wasn't. So, I just stood by the door and waited for what seemed like an eternity. They worked on him at the school, and they continued to work on him in the ambulance and all the way to the hospital. It seemed like it was taking forever. I remember someone telling me that he was coming in, and that his skin color would be blue. They were still trying to revive him. I was in the emergency room when they brought him in. As they worked on him, I held his hand."

As she and I replayed the events of that day, I asked, "You were in the room when the doctors 'called it'?"

"Yes," Mary replied. "I was in the corner of the room for awhile and then I said, 'I need to be with him.' So, I just laid there with him for a while. Jim's mom and dad had to drag me off of him saying 'Mary, you have to leave now.' A close cousin from Chicago heard about Jim's death while I was in the emergency room, and she called the hospital and said 'Let Mary be with Jim as long as she needs to be. You have no idea how close these two were'."

An autopsy performed by the county medical examiner would determine that Jim suffered a sudden cardiac death. No one knew that at the age of thirty-seven, Jim suffered from severe arteriosclerosis or hardening of the arteries.

-----

Most deaths arrive as a thief in the night, unexpectedly robbing us of our loved ones; and as soon as a life is stolen from us, we're expected to complete the laborious task of "making arrangements." During times of celebrations like weddings, a year or more of planning may go into the one day. At death, the announcement to friends and family, the planning of the service, the decisions regarding the interment, the reception after the memorial, all need to be choreographed within just a few short days, all while the next of kin is in a state of shock and confusion.

Laura, one of Mary's sisters-in-law who was an attorney, took the reins of helping with much of the estate settlement work after Jim's death, including drafting and sending out letters regarding potential death proceeds that might be available for Mary and the family. Usually at this point after a client's death, I would have already contacted Mary; but, since the life insurance policy was no longer in force there was nothing to provide; Jim had cancelled his policy.

It's sadly amusing how old documents representing the financial purchases of the past seldom disappear from family file cabinets, even if the product once owned no longer exists. So it was with the life insurance policy Jim had initially acquired through me. The terminated policy hadn't been thrown away. Several weeks had passed since Jim's death when I received a very official looking letter from an attorney, Laura, asking about the details regarding Jim's life insurance policy. That became a very difficult phone call to make.

It was especially difficult when I learned during my telephone call with Laura that the benefits Jim said he had acquired with his new position didn't exist. He had only been employed with the post office for six short months, and the benefits he had told me about had not yet been activated due to the short duration of his employment. The hole we filled with Jim's personally-owned life insurance years earlier was again a void, leaving his family without the replacement of his income, which that policy had been intended to fill. I felt sick and couldn't imagine what his family was experiencing.

-----

Years later, when Mary and I visited about this, she simply said, "We were all surprised, but what are you going to do at that point? You know, there is nothing you can do about it. I honestly do not remember Jim telling me that he cancelled his life insurance policy. It was a complete surprise to me." There were some other smaller policies they owned that allowed Mary to payoff their modest mortgage, but with the extra death benefit missing, there were significant limitations on the family's budget moving forward.

Mary continued on with her life, struggling sometimes to make ends meet. Once her youngsters were in school, she took a job as a cook within the area school district. Health insurance continued to be an expense which was difficult to afford, not being able to put her son and daughter on her own health policy, but having to go out and shop for a lower-priced individual policy for them.

After thirteen years, she remarried, but it wasn't a marriage like the one she had with Jim. Mary admits that her new husband had said that he loved her and wanted to help raise her children. He convinced her she wouldn't have to worry about money anymore because he would take care of her and her children.

"Was it easy for you to be convinced of that?" I asked. "Oh, absolutely," Mary replied, reflecting on years of struggling to get by on only her income. "It was getting to the point where things were getting really tight."

During the next two years, Mary was in a controlling marriage where her new husband tried to take control over her, deciding where they would live, what they would buy, and even who they would have over to their house. "I wasn't allowed to go anywhere," Mary told me. "He bought me a cell phone. He would question why I didn't have my phone with me. Where was I? How long was I there? He had turned into a possessive person, controlling my life."

When that marriage ended, Mary said she had been in a total depression that had really taken her under, but as she walked out of the courtroom that day, Mary noticed that "the trees were greener than green and the sky was bluer than blue."

-----

Reminiscing, yet again about Jim, Mary explained, "We were still on our honeymoon when Jim died. We were still crazy about one another. Like any couple, we had our little fights. After going through an experience like this, I would try and tell young couples to prepare. To be prepared ahead of time is really difficult. I know it was really hard for us, because we both thought we were invincible. We never really talked about insurance. We never really talked about if we should die, because we were only in our mid-thirties."

"If I could speak to a young couple today I would tell them to live every moment to the fullest; get anger out of your life, because that is not going to help. Get the negativity out of your life, because it's too big of a waste. It really is. I was very lucky with Jim. I don't have to look back and say I wish I had done this or I wish I had done that. I was very lucky in that way. We didn't have those fights where you say horrible things to each other. But, I would say today to young couples watch what you say, and watch what you do. Don't piss your money away when you're young. But, try and live your life to its fullest, and yes, be prepared, have wills, and do have life insurance to show your love for each other and your family."

-----

I believe Jim's heart was in the right place. But, I have also experienced through the decades of my career that the lure of quick fixes and believing that there is a simpler, easier, and cheaper way to accomplish your goals are sometimes formidable persuaders that can lure us in a tempting direction that might not be appropriate. This is one of those stories that still pains me to this day. When I was younger, I didn't have the assertiveness I have acquired over time with age and maturity. Had I had those attributes then, maybe this story would have played out differently. Life insurance mirrors life: There isn't an opportunity for a do-over after the fact.

I am blessed that Mary responded when I reached out to her to share Jim's story. Jim's file had been purged from our office records more than two decades ago, though I remembered the pivotal specifics of their lives and how it intertwined with their life insurance decisions.

Here is what you should know: Employee fringe benefits are just that. They are at the fringe of your financial plan. They should not be at the core of your financial security.

Remember the old song? "I owe my soul to the company store," sung by Tennessee Ernie Ford? Individual responsibility trumps employer responsibility. Don't "coast" relying on "the company" to provide for you. This is your responsibility.

I don't care what benefits you have today. Your future benefits package is going to change. How do I know this? Because they have always changed, sometimes for the better, usually for worse. But, they will change. Remember your personally owned benefits like life insurance will only change if you decided to make a change.

My late father-in-law's favorite saying was "Don't confuse them with the facts." Seldom, if ever, does the average person read the details of their benefit package through work. Jim might have believed he actually had the group life insurance. Obviously, he didn't. Jim might have also known about the waiting period before the group life insurance took effect. So, maybe he thought he would simply save the difference in the meantime.

This miscalculation affected his family forever.

Jim made an amateur decision, which really required a professional's advice. Those in my career spend a lot of time reading the small print. The small print is what often determines actual benefits. This isn't a job for an amateur.

-----

After her second marriage, Mary would remain single for the next five years. Because of the wonderful marriage she had with Jim, she knew true happiness could be possible again. It was then that she met Dave. A friend suggested that she connect with Dave, who had lost his own wife ten years earlier. A year earlier he had also lost his son.

Their relationship began slowly with many hours of talking, first by telephone and then in person, taking their time to really get to know one another. They both respected how important their own children were to each other and how much they had both loved their previous spouses, lost through death. Dave's friends would tell him that Mary was "a catch," and Mary's friends said the same about Dave. They were on the same page, held the same values, and shared the same respect for one another. Mary wishes now that she could have met Dave before her second marriage, believing he would have been the right person who could have helped raise her own children with the love and caring they needed.

# Chapter Seven

*"Remember how she was."*

The silent taboo: Suicide. What financial plan includes this possibility?

So far, my career has been touched by suicide on three different occasions. I say "so far," because I am mindful that it may again become something I am called upon to navigate with clients. According to the Center for Disease Control and Prevention (CDC), in 2013, suicide was the tenth leading cause of death for all Americans. Every 13 minutes, a life ends by suicide. The most suicides (19.1 percent of all suicides) are among those between the ages of 45 and 65. The second largest group (18.6 percent of suicides) is among those people over the age of 85. Men are four times more likely than women to commit suicide. More than half of all suicides involve guns.

There was a time when life insurance contracts excluded benefits in the event of death by suicide, but that was nearly a century ago. It was considered an "adverse selection." The exclusion of suicide protected the insurance companies while leaving the beneficiaries with two horrible losses to contend with: first, the loss of someone they loved, and many times, the loss of the support that person might have provided for their family. Today, these provisions have been modified, usually requiring one or two years for the policy to be in effect in order to pay a benefit in the event of a death by suicide.

-----

I met John and Deanne when their lives were filled with future possibilities. He was twenty-seven. She was twenty-five. Deanne was a spitfire with red hair, freckles, a broad smile, and unlimited energy. It was just the two of them then, but they wanted children to be a part of their future together. They already owned a home on a mature tree-lined thoroughfare and they were earnestly set on saving money for their future.

As part of our planning, they decided to increase their life insurance protection by acquiring an additional policy on one another. Several years later, we also added a supplemental disability income policy to cover a shortfall in the employer coverage that Deanne had as an employee with a major medical center in our community. This would provide additional income protection in the event of a disability.

It would be just fourteen years from when they acquired their original life insurance coverage through me to the day John received the phone call alerting him of Deanne's abrupt death.

It's believed that the indirect cause of Deanne's death began years earlier due to an undiagnosed disease. She may have had it for six years, or she might have contracted it fifteen or twenty years earlier, the illness lying dormant all that time, until it erupted in her otherwise healthy body. They never knew. But, after years of an exhaustive search for an answer, it was believed that Deanne was suffering over an extensive period of time with an undiagnosed case of Lyme's disease, carried by a barely visible deer tick.

-----

An adult deer tick is about the size of Franklin Roosevelt's ear on the face of a United States dime. At the time of Deanne's suffering, a test to determine if someone had contracted Lyme's disease was still in its infancy.

According to the CDC, signs and symptoms may include arthritis, facial or Bell's palsy, pain in the tendons, muscles, joints and bones, an irregular heartbeat, dizziness or shortness of breath, inflammation of the brain and spinal cord, nerve pain, shooting pains, numbness, and problems with short-term memory.

Even after this disease is treated, problems with memory or concentration, fatigue, headaches, and sleep disturbances can sometimes persist for the rest of a person's life. The possible fatigue associated with Lyme's disease could be considered on par with that seen in chronic multiple sclerosis patients.

-----

In the beginning, the search for the cause of Deanne's debilitating illness seemed to go on and on, year after year. John and Deanne started to seek advice and treatment outside of the two large medical centers in our community. They finally met a specialist who they felt could provide a nearly certain answer for them, even though it was a time that a diagnosis of Lyme's disease could not yet be 100 percent certain. Nonetheless, the ailments Deanne had suffered had already taken their toll on her life, permanently.

For a few years, the disability policy we acquired for Deanne paid out monthly tax-free income benefits when she could no longer work. But the persistent uncertain causes for her illness limited the length of time her benefits would be paid. John and Deanne also tried to obtain Social Security disability benefits. Those benefits were denied during Deanne's initial request, which is not an unusual occurrence for those familiar with the application process. So, to increase the chances of success, they hired an attorney who specialized in difficult cases such as theirs, to assist them when they reapplied for benefits. It was believed by the Social Security board that Deanne's case was more a situation of depression, than that of Lyme's disease.

Once again, John and Deanne completed all the paperwork, which meant filling out countless government forms. Then, Deanne was interviewed once again trying to receive benefits from a system to which she had paid into her entire adult working life. The attorney said that she had done an excellent job going through the questions the panel had asked, but the request came back denied. Again. By this point, Deanne said to John, "I can't do that again! I cannot go through that process again." She was just too tired and weak. She simply felt she could not jump through the institutional hoops once more.

The last time I saw Deanne in my office she seemed like an eighty-year-old woman, yet she was only half that age, only in her late thirties. She was pale and quiet. Light bothered her; noise bothered her. She would wear dark glasses trying to decrease the brightness of the florescent lights of my office. The day-to-day pain due to her extreme sensitivity was just too much for her to bear.

"It was bizarre," John told me. At that time, "Deanne couldn't leave the bed," he said. "Nor could she even leave the house or walk down the short driveway to retrieve that day's mail. If people would come to check on her during the day, she would keep the garage door opener near her bedside, so she could open it automatically to let people into the house to visit. She was so weak that she couldn't even get up to open the door for them."

This is how the last five years of her life went. John had become a caretaker in addition to his fulltime job while also trying to be a good parent for their two young daughters.

-----

"I remember the day." John said. "It was a Monday. I was attending an after hours Chamber of Commerce event being held at a local bank. I thought to myself about a half hour into it, that there weren't many people I knew and there weren't any customers of mine at the event, so I thought I would simply go home. As I was leaving, one of my customers stopped by late, so I visited with him, then left a little later, picking our girls up from the surround-care we used, on my way home. If I had left when I was first going to leave, Deanne would have been out of the house purchasing the gun that she would use the very next day. So, had I arrived home and she wasn't there, it would have never happened."

Deanne found out about a rideshare program most people would use to keep a doctor's appointment, but she received a ride instead to go to a gun shop. She told the driver that she was so weak, that being home alone, she felt that she needed some kind of protection. She was driven to a gun shop, filled out all the paperwork and waited the five days required to purchase a firearm. The day she went back to pick the gun up was that Monday.

"If I would have come home," John said, "and she wasn't there, I would have immediately known something was wrong and I would have found out about that gun, that day. I didn't know it was there. The gun was in the house that Monday night. It was a .22 pistol."

The police would ask John later, "Why would you have a pistol in the house?" "We don't have a pistol," John exclaimed.

The officers traced the gun back to the gun shop by using the serial number, and then realized that it had just been purchased. The man at the store later said, "I couldn't tell there was anything wrong with her. She seemed perfectly normal."

"So, I think," John continued, "she knew that she was nearing the end and whatever it took to get her there and back, she did it. She filled out the paperwork without making a mistake. She had her driver's license with her for identification and had the money to make the purchase. She signed everything and went to pick up the gun five days later. She then took a few instructions on how to use it. The store employee said she was perfectly fine."

"She hid it under the bed," John continued. "If the kids would have been playing or if something had rolled under there...." His sentence drifted off and then he continued, "Had I known it was there, it would have freaked me out."

-----

The day after Deanne purchased the gun, John left work, picked up the girls, who were then eight and six years old, from their after school surround-care program and took them to their softball games.

John would later learn of a note that was left by Deanne on their bedroom door: "John, please take the girls out of the house and call the police."

The Lutheran church they attended has a parish nurse named Linnea, who would do blood pressure checks after Sunday services and sometimes she would make home visits to congregational members. Deanne may have reached out one last time on that day, as she tried to call their parish nurse. Sadly, Linnea's cell phone wasn't answered and so the voice message didn't arrive until later.

The softball games ended for the girls, and they were soon on their way home.

Remembering as if it had just happened yesterday, John continued "So, I'm coming down our street and as I turn the corner, I see two county sheriff cars in our driveway; and as soon as my car was straight in its lane, after making the turn onto our street, at that very moment my phone rings. It was our parish nurse."

"I'm sorry to tell you this, John," Linnea said from the other end of the line, "but Deanne has passed away."

John continued, "I'm literally driving by our house as Linnea is talking to me. I just kept driving. I'm replying to her 'okay,' then pausing to listen and then again saying 'okay,' all the while driving and then from the backseat the girls ask me 'What's going on?' I just kept driving and told them that Mom had fallen and hurt her foot and the police were there to help to get her to the hospital and I had to go to the hospital."

"Fortunately, a neighbor of ours, Tammy, was still at the softball game, as I returned to the ball diamonds," John said. "I walked up to her and asked 'Can you watch the kids?' I told her that Deanne had hurt herself and I needed to go home. She looked at me, while I gave a distressed nod. Tammy's eyes began to tear up."

"When I pulled up to the house, the sheriff's deputies were coming out and told me what had happened and that our church nurse had identified the body. So, I didn't have to go in," John expressed his relief.

"When I left that night at about ten o'clock, our neighbor Bill, who is a police officer came over to the house and spoke with the other police officers. They took the mattress away and got rid of everything else. So, when we came back, the room was clean. To this day, I thank Bill for that. They got everything out of there."

One of the coroners asked John, "What did Deanne do for a living?"

"She did echo cardiographs—heart ultrasounds," John replied. "That explains it," the coroner continued. "She knew what she was doing, because with a .22 pistol, suicide is a hard thing to do. It's not like it was a shotgun." With an uncomfortable assurance in her voice, the coroner said, "It had to be quick. It had to be."

-----

John's dad called Deanne's parents.

The hardest thing for John was telling their girls about their mom's death. "When I picked them up," he said, "they already knew their mother had died, though we didn't say how. My mother, their grandmother, had picked them up at the park and sat with them that evening."

Now, John was faced with planning his wife's funeral the very next day. As they talked, their minister said to John, "The girls are going to hear that Deanne shot herself. It's going to come out. People are going to talk at the funeral. You've got to go home and tell the girls what happened." "But, they're just eight and six years old," John said with frustration in his voice. "Yes," their minister said. "But, you have to tell them, today."

"The worst conversation I've ever had in my life was when I had to tell our daughters how their mother died. I don't ever want to do anything like that ever again. They didn't process it, right away. There were a lot of tears and a lot of 'whys'. That was a hard day. That was a very hard day." As John reflected, he continued "But, you do come through it. There is a light at the end of the tunnel."

John remembered, "There was a time, I don't know if it was during the funeral or afterwards, because it was all such a blur. But, there was a moment when the lead pastor of our church, said 'John, I need you for five minutes'." As they stood together, his pastor continued, "For what it's worth, you have two options right now. On Monday morning you're going to get a phone bill or you're going to get an electric bill or you're going to get a credit card bill," he said. "The world goes on. You can choose to go through the world and be bitter and angry and mad; but, it's still going to go on, all around you, and your world could become smaller, because no one will want to be around you; or you can choose to go out into the world, figure out what happened. And no one is going to like what happened, but you have to think of your girls and go through the day as positive as you can, and the rest will fall into place.'"

Looking up at me as he recounted his pastor's words years later, John nodded and said, "He was right."

-----

As I viewed the photos of Deanne with groups of her friends and family, placed on large placards against the wall in the fellowship area of their church prior to her funeral service, John stepped up to me and said something that I still recall today. It seemed at that moment, as if John was the one consoling us, when we should have been the ones consoling him.

He said, "Remember the Deanne that you see in those pictures. Remember how she was."

The photos illustrated Deanne's life. But, in the array of pictures, John made certain that several recent photos were also included, so everyone could see that there was a visibly distressing change that caused Deanne's life to end as it had.

No one makes plans to die a decade or more in advance of a suicide. In fact, if I were to ask for a show of hands, few of us plan on death at all, of any kind. It's something we all would rather deny. But, it happens nonetheless.

I find the process of completing death claim forms in nearly any situation to be a heart-wrenching experience. Deanne's death ended years of pain she had suffered through, which the rest of us regrettably will never fully understand.

John remembered that after we completed the insurance paperwork, I had suggested that he check his mailbox each day after about a week and a half, for the death claim to arrive. "I came home one day for lunch," said John, "and when I saw it, I starting thinking to myself, 'I've got two kids. I don't know how my job is going to be affected by this. Plus, I'm in sales and they want me to travel. I should just pay off the house.' So, when I saw the amount, I simply drove right to the bank. The teller asked if I wanted to make a deposit. 'No'," he continued. "I want to pay off my mortgage. A banker took me into a smaller room and I wrote a check from the insurance claim account, and the mortgage was over and done with."

The life insurance proceeds John received provided certainty of financial stability during a time of family uncertainty. But, that too would also change.

-----

It was New Year's Eve of that year; John attended a party at the home of his neighbors, Bill and Tammy. John didn't want to be there at midnight, so he thanked Tammy for inviting him before it got too late. He said that he probably wasn't the best guest, but thanked them nonetheless. Before he left, Tammy confronted John by asking, "You probably don't want to hear this, but are you ready to date again?" "No, no," John said, and then he continued, "No, Tammy, there's no way." She replied, "There's someone who knows us, and they know that we know you; they may have someone you might be interested in. And when it feels right," she said, "maybe you should let us know." John answered, "When it feels right, sure; but, not now."

The woman to whom Tammy was referring was Kate.

Nearly a year later, Kate was attending a local Rotary Club meeting and was visiting with another friend, Sue, who was also the wife of the contractor who built John and Deanne's house. Sue asked Kate if she would be interested in meeting a friend of hers.

Sue continued, "Here's the story. There's this dad, widowed with two daughters. He may be interested or he might not be, but you should meet him."

Kate responded, "This is the second time, I've heard about this guy, what are the odds?" Then she continued, "A woman I work with mentioned this guy to me, too; and they asked him in December and he said he wasn't ready." Sue said, "I'll make a call anyway, just a call." So, as John would remember, "Out of the blue, I received this email from Sue."

-----

John had gone on one date by this time that a friend had set up. It was his first in more than fifteen years. He said that it was uncomfortable and awkward. John admitted that he had forgotten how to go on dates, and that the experience left him somewhat uncomfortable about future attempts. That was about the time John received Sue's email. Replying, he told Sue that her timing was good. He had just gone on that first date, but he didn't know how good he was at this "dating thing." Still, he answered, "Sure, set it up."

"I actually called Kate the week of her birthday," John shared. Continuing he remembered what he said: "This is John. Sue gave me your name. If you're interested in going out, I would love to meet you." Kate asked if the kids were up and John said that they were already in bed for the night. John said it was very natural and relaxed, as they visited. They talked for nearly an hour.

With the ease of that initial conversation, they set up a date for that very weekend, enjoying dinner at an Italian restaurant, walking along a riverside park and finishing the evening by having a drink together, before John took her home. They spent the whole time during that first date talking. "The date," John said, "went well."

For their second date, John invited his neighbors Sue and Jim to join them for spaghetti at his house and when they left, Kate lingered afterward as she and John continued talking. Kate would ask questions like "How are the girls?" and "How did you get through this?" Their relationship just snowballed. John would often go to Kate's house, sitting outside on the deck with her, and they would just talk.

John acknowledged, "It just felt right."

After meeting John's girls, after they started getting to the point when they began to seriously think about marriage, Kate said to John, "I feel Deanne put me here for your kids."

"She's been a great mom," John continued. "Never having any children, she walked in, and took over; even though there might have been some bumps, as happens with any teenagers."

Along the way, John and Kate added a third daughter to their family.

-----

I asked John how the girls handled the loss of their mother. The eldest missed her mom a lot and would sometimes cry at night, and John or Kate would go and lay beside her for comfort. The younger of the two remembered that her mom was sick, because one day she asked for a piggyback ride, and her mother couldn't give her one. She never got another piggyback ride.

One of John's ministers said to him that "on the day of the suicide there were two people in the room. There was the Deanne we knew; and then there was not-Deanne. The Deanne we knew fought for as long as she could."

John shared, "I remember after her remains were interred and I would stop and visit her gravesite on her birthday or on our anniversary. It was the middle of the week, during one visit. I stood there and it was very, very quiet. I blocked out the nearby noise of street traffic. It was silent and I said 'Okay God, I just need to know, is she in heaven? Could you give me a bird singing, could you give me any little noise?'"

As soon as he finished that thought, the bell tower at the nearby university rang out, a tower and bells John never knew were there. That provided the reassurance he needed.

"The life insurance was instrumental in how we got through this, financially, as a family," John shared. "Deanne and I lived through seven years of hell through her sickness, together. In the beginning, she still worked and then the last five years it became progressively worse. We were chopping her food in a food processor, because she couldn't chew. She could barely go to the bathroom by herself. At one time, I wondered if we should be considering nursing home care, but I simply couldn't bring myself to that. I would come home from working a full day, get the kids and then do the grocery shopping. We would grab McDonald's; go home, and I would make sure the kids finished their homework. If they needed a birthday gift for a party, I made sure it happened. I tried to make sure that they felt no effect to their lives."

"I remember one night, when Deanne had a neighbor over to watch the girls and put them to bed. It was Christmas. I went out. It was a cold and dark winter night and I was out alone. I remember going through a grocery store at eleven-thirty at night; and the lady at the checkout, looked at me and asked quietly, 'Would you like me to help you bag your groceries?' 'God bless you, yes'," John replied. "I can't imagine how I looked. But, remember I didn't go through anything—not like Deanne had. Whatever bumps I experienced along the way were nothing."

-----

John remembered something I had said to him years earlier when visiting with him and Deanne. He repeated it back to me. "You buy this, this life insurance, hoping that you'll never need it, but you'll never know when you might."

John relived a conversation he and Deanne had together years earlier, out loud for my benefit.

"Deanne," he said. "Look at what we're doing here. We're spending this money and we're getting life insurance. Our friends are traveling. Why should we buy this?" "Because it makes sense," she said. John agreed by saying "Okay," not even realizing the impact it would someday make.

The life insurance that Deanne felt strongly about years earlier provided the security for Kate to work part-time enabling her to be at home with all three girls, as they have gone through their school years. Deanne and John's decision to own the asset of life insurance continues to ripple through their family's life yet today helping to provide security for the family and giving their daughters the opportunity of debt-free college educations.

-----

I have several good friends who are ministers who have shared the following Bible verse with me when they're asked about the theological complications of trying to understand suicide. It may provide some peace and the hope of God's gentle hand of reassurance.

"Who shall separate us from the love of Christ? Shall tribulation, or distress, or persecution, or famine, or nakedness or peril, or sword?" (Romans 9:35 KJV)

Investments Don't Hug

# Chapter Eight

*Term Insurance*

"A house is probably the single largest investment you will ever make during your lifetime."

Not true; though for many people it may be "the single largest asset acquired during their lifetime."

An investment and an asset are not necessarily the same thing. An investment is something that pays you money. Unfortunately, as every homeowner knows, a house costs money every single month you own it, even after it's paid for! The upkeep doesn't end, nor do the real estate taxes and homeowners' insurance. A house is an asset; but, it's definitely not an investment.

Betty and I knew when we were first married that homeownership would be an eventual goal of ours. We approached the conservative purchase of our first home in a very systematic way, having already rented the bottom half of an old yellow house that had been converted into a duplex by a schoolteacher and his wife. It was situated on the main thoroughfare of a small farming community of thirteen thousand people in the middle of southern Minnesota where we began our careers. It was a very old house that had settled on its foundation over the years. The floor of the kitchen pitched at a slight angle, and it seemed that if you dropped something round onto the floor, it would probably roll downhill. One of the bedrooms had outdated multi-tone blue shag carpeting, but instead of gracing the floor, it covered a wall while the other three were covered with complementing blue flock wallpaper, which had the texture of stiff velvet.

-----

After several years of living surrounded by the rich black farmland of the flat prairie, we moved to a larger college community situated along the Mississippi River overlooked by Minnesota bluffs to the west and Wisconsin bluffs to the east. When we arrived in town, the options for rentals had been thoroughly picked over by the student population attending the state university, two private colleges and a vocational school. I remembered the frustration of learning there were only a handful of rental possibilities for us in the small city of thirty-five thousand people. We felt trapped in the two-story brick apartment complex we were able to find at the last minute. It fit our budget, but we felt like rats trapped in a cage with the lack of outdoor living space we had become accustomed to and the stark white-painted hallways leading to our apartment, with its layout identical to every other apartment in the cookie-cutter building.

As renters, we were shelling out money every single month with nothing to show for it, except another rent payment due the following month. In the most simplistic analogy, renting is like buying term life insurance. This isn't an opinion of whether renting is good or bad, nor is it an opinion of whether term life insurance is good or bad. Every situation is unique at the time the decision is contemplated. Early in our marriage we rented, because it was the appropriate decision for that time in our lives, which centered around two realities: we had very little money, and we were still too young to begin thinking about the eventual direction we were going to take in our early careers and as a family—it was still just the two of us, without the responsibility that comes along with children.

-----

So, in the early years of our marriage, just as we rented a place to live, we also owned substantial amounts of term insurance, because it was the appropriate decision for that particular time in our lives. We rented our home. We also rented our term insurance.

You may ask, why am I referring to renting our term insurance at that time in our lives. "Didn't you buy it, Mark?"

Not really, buying implies "ownership," and contractually, we were purchasing our term life insurance for a "term of time," similar to the term of a lease for the apartment we rented.

When advisors, insurance companies, or financial media personalities promote without any question whatsoever, that term insurance is better than permanent life insurance or that permanent life insurance is better than term life insurance, they are providing an opinion without delving intimately into the particular situation of the individual seeking advice. Giving an absolute determination as to the "only appropriate kind of life insurance product" without regard to an individual's circumstances shows ignorance. When I am asked which product I believe is the best choice over another, my answer can initially leave the person frustrated when I default to the answer of "it depends."

-----

Term and permanent life insurance products are very different from one another and should be used in different situations and under different circumstances, which will ultimately provide different final results. Our own family has owned a lot of term insurance. We have also owned a combination of term and permanent life insurance. As of the writing of this book, our current portfolio of life insurance policies is exclusively permanent insurance. Why has there been an evolution in our life insurance strategies? Because our lives have continued to change and evolve, and permanent life insurance is the appropriate choice for what we wish to accomplish with our money, especially what I consider to be our "safe" money.

As this book delves into the discussion of different types of life insurance policies, it's easiest to begin the conversation with term life insurance. The reason term life insurance is sold so aggressively by phone, by mail, and over the internet is that it is thought to be the least complicated type of life insurance to explain; and it also helps that it's *initially* the least expensive to purchase. The sales pitch for term life insurance is pretty straight forward: "It's cheap." But, the reality is not as clear cut as many agents and their prospective clients would like to believe. The simplicity surrounding term life insurance begins and ends with the simple math about its initial cost.

Everything else being equal, term insurance for a thirty-year-old person is cheaper than that for a forty-year-old, and obviously cheaper than that for someone who is fifty or sixty. The farther you are away from your own personal "expiration date," the less expensive the policy should be. Mathematically it's also less likely to payout a claim. Here's an interesting fact—the life insurance companies know it too.

Decades ago, most life insurance companies only offered a single standard version of term insurance. It was referred to as an ART or an Annual Renewal Term policy. These policies are seldom seen today. Yet, these old style policies may have been fairer to the insured, because they were priced in "real time."

Each year the policy's pricing was adjusted based on your underwriting classification. If you were a healthy thirty-year-old male when you initially purchased the policy, the premium would be adjusted the next year, based in part on the insurance company's experience during the previous year for all healthy thirty-year-old males they insured in their "class" or classification. There would be a gradual and predictable increase in the price curve of the insurance over time, as your "class" neared the common age of expected mortality (i.e. death) and, of course, also based on your particular company's actual death claims, administrative expenses, and investment performance.

If the insurance company outperformed the industry's average cost, you may be rewarded by more stable premiums from year to year; or if you had a dividend paying policy from a contract issued through a mutual insurance company, an expected policy premium increase might be offset by a dividend declared and used to reduce your annual premium. (We'll discuss mutual companies and dividends in an upcoming chapter.)

But, with the advent of direct marketing, insurance companies began to redesign their products to have a more competitive pricing structure to provide a promotional advantage to increase sales. Whenever an insurance company introduces a new policy design, the first question I ask myself is "What is the company taking away from their policy design to achieve its new competitive pricing advantage, and is it really in a client's best interest?"

This may provide some perspective about my concerns regarding the aggressive advertising of short-duration term insurance products. When I see a cinematically produced television ad featuring a young couple enjoying a summer picnic together in a tree-lined park with their two young children who appear to be about four and six years of age nearby and a genteel voice of an announcer explains how this caring father purchased a half million dollars of level ten-year term life insurance coverage for less than the price of a daily donut and coffee each month, I immediately become angry with the television, because I know something an unsuspecting parent who wants to do the correct thing for his family doesn't understand.

There is no disclaimer showing that:

- His policy may end or have a substantial price increase in premiums; so large in fact, that after the first ten years of owning this policy, he may be left without his initial insurance protection altogether.
- If his health changes after his original policy is purchased, he could be denied new coverage on a new policy, at the very time his children are fourteen and sixteen years of age.
- His policy could expire before he does, and he won't realize the mistake he made until it is too late.

Remember, at the time when this "picture-perfect" couple first applied for their term life insurance policies, the life insurance company reviewed all their doctor's medical records. The company probably also had an examiner perform a blood test and a urinalysis; height and weight measurements were evaluated, and perhaps even an EKG was completed. After checking this couple out thoroughly and approving their applications for ten years of level term insurance, the insurance company can be relatively confident that the odds of death over the course of the next decade are going to be in the insurance company's statistical favor. They hold most of the cards. In this game of poker, the house almost always wins.

Remember, if you reapply for a brand new ten-year term insurance policy a decade later when your current policy expires, the insurance company is allowed to revisit and reevaluate whether you qualify once again for the next go-a-round with term insurance. The decision of what the new premium will be and whether, based on your current health, you can even obtain the new policy, is out of your hands. The decision is for the insurance company to make, because the initial contract price of the ten-year term insurance ended at the end of those first ten years.

When we're young and healthy, we all just assume that ten years later we're going to be just a little bit older and that we're going to be just as healthy as we are today. If that were indeed the fact, why would you even consider buying life insurance at all? It sounds like you don't need it. Unfortunately, with age comes one undeniable truth about your health: with each passing birthday—just like a car—all the original equipment begins to break down, no matter how often you take it into the shop and have a mechanic check under the hood. We go to our annual medical examinations hoping for suggestions on how to stay fit and healthy. But, with age it seems to become more of an annual documentation of what's wearing out and of how healthy we "were" the previous year.

When purchasing term life insurance, look for a policy that has a conversion privilege. All of our futures are uncertain, so you want as many options available as possible. A conversion privilege is an option to convert your present term insurance policy into a permanent insurance policy, using whatever age you are when you elect to take advantage of this privilege in the future. The key element is that you can still qualify with the exact same health classification as when you obtained the initial term policy. It doesn't matter if you now have high blood pressure or are diabetic or have had a heart attack.

So, when purchasing a term insurance policy some important questions worth asking are: Is this policy convertible and if so, for how long; and if I do convert it in the future, what are my options for permanent insurance coverage?

-----

Death is a sure thing. Yet, some of us want to cheat death or at least cheat the cost of death. That's the way it is with term life insurance. The thinking is that you could cheat death today at a lower cost, by betting against it, assuming that your chance of not dying is better than the average individual. Using the actuarial tables provided by the Social Security Administration (Period Life Table—2013), the chance of a thirty-year-old man dying by the time he reaches the age of sixty-five is only seventeen percent. That means the chance of that same man being alive at age sixty-five is a wonderful eighty-three percent! Most men (and women) believe their chances of living are even greater, because of their own good eating habits, available healthcare, and fulfilling lives. So, it wouldn't be unusual for you to believe that your chance of being alive at the age of sixty-five to be at least ninety percent or greater with only a ten percent chance or less of dying prior to that retirement age. In fact, let's be brutally honest, you probably believe that your own chance of dying before reaching the age of sixty-five is near zero, right?

If that's the case, there's now a huge hole in the argument to buying term insurance. If you believed that there is only a limited chance of dying prior to your normal retirement age, why would you spend money on buying term life insurance to insure your life for only that limited term of time? Sounds like a poor financial decision. But, you might have wanted to buy term life insurance, "just in case."

Here's the ugly mathematical truth: if you reach the age of sixty-five, in all likelihood your personal "just in case" term insurance has expired and any fringe benefits of term life insurance coverage through your employer was terminated when you left your job. So now you are without life insurance, which could have insured your Human Life Value, at exactly the time when you have come to the realization that your chance of dying in the future is now one hundred percent!

None of us is getting out of here alive, and if you were to die two weeks, two months or two years after the expiration of your term life insurance, not only is your spouse going to be "a little ticked at your financial timing," but think of what should have been passed on to your loved ones that wasn't, because of the cheap financial decision you made to try and cheat the cost of death.

If given the choice, would you rather be wrong a fraction of the time—owning permanent life insurance and dying too soon, or owning momentary term life insurance and living too long?

I have sat with countless families, attorneys and accountants after a client's death and never, ever, during my entire career have I been asked what kind of life insurance my client owned. The only two questions I have been asked are "How much?" and "How soon?" How much life insurance was there, and how soon will the insurance company pay the proceeds. I remember the conversation coming up even at my own grandfather's wake after he passed away in his mid-eighties, just a couple of weeks following the birth of my son. I overheard someone ask, "Did he have any life insurance?" That was two decades after what was considered his normal retirement age.

If none of us can cheat death, wouldn't you want to embrace an asset you can own and control for your whole life and then, when your final day arrives, pass on to the ones you love?

Investments Don't Hug

# Chapter Nine

*"If they say you're disabled, you're no good to me."*

It happened during the night as Robbie was sleeping. The days before he had been working on the fire suppression system in the attic of a nursing home. Working for the same company for twenty-six years, the master plumber wanted to retire in six years at the age of fifty-seven. That evening when he arrived home, he was more tired than usual, dehydrated from spending the day between the ceiling and the roof of the care facility. He just didn't feel right and simply needed to lie down for the night. His wife, Lisa, remembers: "We had supper. The evening was no different than any other."

"The next day, Robbie was going through his regular early morning routine," Lisa said. "But, he was banging into the walls."

"What the heck are you doing?" she asked, only comprehending his peculiar expression and slurred speech as he struggled to even stir his coffee.

Something had happened. "We should have called 911 right away," Lisa said. "But, we didn't."

Despite a desperate rush through at least one red light, by the time they reached the hospital the stroke had run its course. The damage was done.

Robbie spent the next two days in the hospital. The stroke affected the left side of his body, and since he was left-handed, penmanship became difficult and his writing was hard to read. Initially his left foot didn't work either. His leg did, but not his foot. The damage caused by the stroke also affected the left side of his peripheral vision.

"For the longest time," Lisa said, "Robbie would bump into things. The first year is the most important time with a stroke, because after the first year, if improvements haven't been made, they won't be made any longer."

While some effects of the stroke would improve with therapy, Robbie's life was permanently changed.

-----

The stroke forced Robbie to retire six years ahead of schedule. The medical term of his lasting impairment is vascular dementia—better stated, he has difficulty with his short-term memory.

"I did go back to work for a while," said Robbie, "maybe a month." But the short-term memory lapses left him wondering at times if he had thoroughly completed a project, and worried that he would overlook something important. It was a hard blow to take when his doctor and employer confirmed what he feared.

"The doctors confirmed that he couldn't work again," Lisa said, "and John, Robbie's employer simply said, 'Take the retirement Robbie. If they say you're disabled, you're no good to me.'"

"The company lost a big part of their business in our area because of your stroke," Lisa pointed out, with Robbie sitting beside her. Robbie was able to receive his pension early because of his disability, but it wasn't as large as it would have been had he been able to work those additional six years. Staying upbeat and also realizing many people don't have pensions at all to fall back on, Robbie said, "You don't know what life is going to throw at you. You could be dead tomorrow."

"Robbie continued through a lot of cognitive testing," Lisa continued, "At first we wouldn't believe his condition was really as bad as it was. But, after five or six doctors, we thought, forget it."

They came to terms with the cards they had been dealt.

"The back of the right side of the brain is where your memory works," Lisa explained. "The blockage created from the traveling plaque in Robbie's blood vessels had already passed by the time we arrived at the hospital." Robbie's short-term memory was affected the most. "I find it harder to concentrate on things," he said. "Sometimes he forgets that the kitchen stove is on," Lisa added.

-----

The year before Robbie's disability, they could not have imagined that their life could become any worse. Robbie and Lisa had lost their house due to a flood caused by a torrential rainfall. In mid-August, flooding of historic proportions occurred in the upper Mississippi River valley with more than twelve inches of rain coming down on a Saturday night continuing into the early hours of the next morning. The flood damaged the foundation of their home, literally tilting it to one side. They could save only half of what they owned. Nine inches of water soaked into everything that was low to the floor. Luckily, everything from the bottom drawers of cabinets and dressers on up was salvaged.

Their house itself was a total loss and had to be completely rebuilt. "We had just gotten done with the flood and moved back into the house in May, and then Robbie had the stroke on July third," recalled Lisa. "That first year, I thought, my God, how are we going to do this? We're going to be eating in the soup lines."

Yet, almost always upbeat, she continued. "But other people have it worse than we do. You just have to go with the flow. You just keep going forward," she said. "What are you going to do, lie down and die? You just go with it and with a lot of prayers."

It was another year after Robbie gave up his attempt to return to work before Social Security benefits would kick in. Our office managed Robbie's retirement account from his employer to begin providing a monthly income, and I remember bringing to their attention a "waiver of premium" benefit they had included on Robbie's whole life insurance policies. "If it weren't for you," Lisa mentioned to me later, "we wouldn't have even realized that Robbie had that benefit. You were the one person to bring it to our attention."

The process of receiving the insurance company's waiver of premium benefit took a much shorter period of time than their wait for the Social Security Administration to approve Robbie's benefits. "It was much more difficult to apply for the Social Security disability" Lisa remarked. "In fact, it took about six months just to get the paperwork together to apply for the government benefits."

Why was it important to include a "waiver of premium" benefit on Robbie's whole life insurance policies? Initially, it sounds like the only benefit of having it was to eliminate the need of having to pay ongoing premiums for a life insurance policy in the event of a disability. But, it's actually a whole lot more than that.

In the event of a disability, there is typically a waiting period of four to six months before the benefit begins. You may think of this as a 'deductible'. Once the initial period has passed and the insurance company has approved the claim, the life insurance policy continues just as if the insured were paying the premiums themselves, except that the insurance company is paying the premiums for you.

That means the insured's policy continues to receive all the scheduled guaranteed cash reserve increases and any declared dividends which the policy is entitled to earn each year, as they are declared. Many companies also refund any premiums which were paid during the initial waiting or 'deductible' period.

"If it weren't for you, we wouldn't be where we are today financially, Mark," Lisa said.

-----

I reviewed my own office death claim statistics recently. More than two-thirds of the life insurance policies that have resulted in death claims, or those which will result in imminent death claims, have been or are currently being paid by the insurance company and not the insured through the benefit of a 'waiver of premium' rider.

If this benefit is included on a term insurance policy, there typically are one of three possible options for how this benefit can be used, depending on the contract language of the particular life insurance company issuing the policy.

First: The premiums are paid, but no conversion option is available to change the contract to a whole life insurance policy.

This means the insurance company pays the premium of the term insurance policy, so the insured will not experience any cost or expense moving forward. But, no changes or improvements to the policy can be made. If the insured wants to upgrade or convert the term policy to a permanent life insurance policy in the future, he or she will have to pay the premiums on the new policy, and if the current policy has a set date when it expires, the insured could be left with no coverage at all.

Second: The premiums are paid and a future paid conversion is available.

This means that the insurance company will pay the current premiums for the term insurance policy and will allow the conversion or upgrade of the policy at a set future date, at which time, the insurance company will pay for the increased premiums which will build equity or cash reserves inside the policy, at the company's expense, but the insurance company is in charge of the timing of this conversion, which typically may not occur until the age of sixty-five.

Third: The premiums are paid, with the timing of a possible conversion or upgrade to permanent life insurance, such as a whole life policy, determined by the insured.

If the term insurance policy is operating under a waiver of premium benefit, the company is obligated to begin to immediately pay for the upgraded or converted policy with its substantially higher new premium, when the insured decides to exercise this option. This choice provides the most flexibility and potentially the greatest benefits for the insured and for the beneficiary.

If an individual is permanently disabled with the third waiver of premium option it's important to realize that there are two very important reasons to convert this policy as soon as possible. First, if the insured is expected to live for some years into the future, a 'participating' whole life policy which uses its annual declared dividends to purchase additional paid-up insurance could increase the eventual death benefit to the beneficiaries without any additional out-of-pocket cost of the insured. I have personally used this option in my practice and have seen the additional benefits passed on to a loved one's family.

Another reason to use this benefit is to enhance an insured's retirement strategies due to a permanent disability that may have ended their working years early. When a disability occurs, but doesn't end in death, it can sometimes feel worse than death. Often, if there is a disability income plan through the employee's place of work, it may only provide up to two-thirds of what their earnings were prior to the beginning of the disability.

In addition, this employer disability benefit is almost always integrated with government benefits of Social Security and/or worker's compensation, which means the disability benefits through an employer are reduced by the amount of those benefits received through any government program. You typically can't receive both. Likewise, in nearly every possible scenario, both the employee and the employer contributions cease for pension or 401(k) contributions; and with a new lower household income due to the disability, it is very unlikely money will be available to invest for a future retirement, because the future retirement is now—today—taken on as a disability instead.

Robbie and Lisa didn't have to be concerned with whether the insurance they owned was term insurance which would have been needed to be converted, because Robbie's insurance was all permanent whole life insurance and was already building equity or cash reserves with guaranteed cash value increases and dividends that could be declared annually by the insurance company. Both Lisa and Robbie agreed that their only mistake was probably not having more insurance with a higher premium, which would have become the responsibility of the insurance company after Robbie's disability.

-----

Robbie's life expectancy will probably be the same as if he had never had a stroke. What was really shortened was Robbie's *earning* life expectancy. All new contributions to his future ended at the moment of his stroke, except for the contributions (i.e. premiums) made by his life insurance company towards his whole life insurance policy. Remember, the only thing that changes with a disability under a waiver of premium benefit is who pays the premium: guaranteed cash values increase, dividends continue to be paid on participating policies, as declared by the company, and loans can still be secured by the insured. The difference is that the insured can put away their checkbook because the premium payments are no longer their responsibility.

Knowing the outcome of a possible disability, which would you rather have?

- A life insurance policy with a waiver of premium benefit or one without?
- A term life insurance policy which you could convert to a permanent life insurance policy on your timeline, paid by the insurance company,

or one converted at the choice, timing, and whim of the insurance company?

- And if you were to become disabled, would you want to have the lowest possible premium, providing you with the lowest possible accumulation of equity or cash reserve benefits, or would you want to have the highest possible premium, which could provide you with the highest possible accumulation of equity or cash reserve benefits?

Here's something the public and, in fact, many insurance agents would find useful to learn, as well. During the underwriting process to acquire life insurance, not only is the insurance company interested in knowing the circumstances of your health history, but they also want to know about your financial history. In fact, insurance companies have established limits as to how much they will allow you to put in (i.e. pay) toward a life insurance policy on an ongoing (annual) basis.

Think about this. Why would they even care? Wouldn't more be better for them? It probably would be. The real answer revolves around the concept of "insurable interest." If you own a permanent whole life insurance policy and become disabled, which would mean that you no longer have to pay premiums, would the insurance company rather you have a large annual premium policy or a small annual premium policy?

If you were to become disabled which would you rather have, a big premium that has the potential to build big future values or a small premium that would potentially build smaller future values? In the event of a disability, which do you think the insurance company would prefer you to have?

Which would you rather have?

Investments Don't Hug

# Chapter Ten

*"I thought it was stupid for them to do it."*

Perspective helps. Time and experiences often change our original perceptions. It had been nearly eight years since Shelley's death at the age of thirty-six, when I sat across from her daughter in the basement family room of her grandparent's home. Kaitlyn had just graduated from high school and was looking forward to attending college in the fall. I was struck by the similarities of mother and daughter, especially when Kaitlyn smiled. It almost seemed as if I was visiting a dear friend, who I had not seen in a long while.

Shelley was twenty-five years old and was seven months pregnant with Kaitlyn when she applied for life insurance on an early August evening.

Other than the anticipated weight gain of an expectant mother, Shelley was otherwise healthy. I learned though, that Shelley's husband, Jason, had a heart condition. But, I didn't realize then how serious it was; I learned later that as time went on in Jason's life, he could very well become a transplant candidate. For now, medication kept him healthy; unfortunately, however, not healthy enough to receive an approval for life insurance coverage.

Sometimes it's mistakenly believed by the public that getting a life insurance policy is easy. It is relatively simple to apply for life insurance. Yet, it's an altogether different story as to whether you'll be approved to receive it. Advertising would have you believe that there are multiple pricing structures available, depending on how good your health might be. However, for simplicity's sake, in my experience the application outcome generally falls to three possible conclusions:

- Approval of the application, as applied for;
- Rated: meaning because of poor health there is a ongoing surcharge; or
- Declined: in which the insurance company simply returns your initial premium and says, "Sorry, but no thank you."

Jason received a "Sorry, but no thank you" letter; Shelley though, was approved, as applied for.

-----

Sometimes young married couples will seek out parental advice when making some of those first "adult" decisions on their own, fearful of making a costly mistake and thinking they can lean on the experience of those who have been there before.

My wife, Betty, and I felt that same way when we were first married. Often times, we would seek out the guidance and advice of my father-in-law, especially when buying our first home. Betty had lived in thirteen different communities during her childhood, since her dad was a corporate-climber for International Multifoods, which required a move with each new promotion. Who would be better to ask than Bill for his advice on buying a house? He had bought more houses than anyone I had ever known.

Regrettably though, some advice is based only on an opinion. That is usually the case with insurance—any kind of insurance—and especially, life insurance. Just a few short moments prior to my conversation with Kaitlyn, I was upstairs in the kitchen having a cup of coffee and listening to what Shelley's mother, Kathy, had told her only child, Shelley, eighteen years earlier. I was hearing this story first hand for the first time. I was stunned.

-----

When Kathy found out that Shelley had made the purchase of life insurance, she told me, "I thought it was stupid for them to do it. I've never been a life insurance person."

"I was wrong, and I will be the first to admit it," she told me, with the wisdom of hindsight.

What had particularly frustrated Kathy at the time was that Jason was the one with the medical issues. In theory, he was the one most likely to die, not Shelley. "And that's what irritated me more than anything," Kathy said.

"Now they are paying premiums on Shelley," she recalls thinking, "and yet she's going to end up with nothing if something happens to Jason. You know what I'm saying?"

"I didn't even know they were doing it (buying the life insurance). It was already over and done with before I knew; and it's a good thing too, because I probably would have talked them out of it," Kathy said.

"So, had you had your way," I interrupted, "Kaitlyn would have had nothing."

Kathy answered back. "But, that's what upset me more than anything. Because I thought Shelley was going to be left with nothing; and yet, they were paying life insurance premiums on her; and for what, I was asking myself? Little did I know", she said.

Shelley's dad, Bud, who had been relatively silent up until that point of our conversation, suddenly spoke up. "The one thing you can put in your book," he said, "if you have any young couples that don't think life insurance is important when they're young and don't want to spend the money, they'd better! That was just like us. We both had decent jobs and I thought, 'I ain't putting my money in no life insurance policy. We're going to save it!'"

He had come to the realization that he and his wife were wrong, and their daughter Shelley was right.

In fact, what they didn't realize is that they could have had both: a place to park their safe money, while owning a protective death benefit along the way.

-----

# Chapter Ten

Shelley's death came within a month of the ten-year anniversary of when she and Jason had met with me to apply for that life insurance policy. They had only been married a short time when they applied for the insurance, and were expecting their first born. Somehow, they did the right thing, the mature thing. They had a limited budget, but they put first things, first. They both realized this is what responsible people do.

Shelley's death years later wasn't quick; it was drawn out. The journey began with an unexpected seizure. Medical tests indicated brain cancer. There were times of triumph when Shelley's doctor believed she was freed from this malignancy. There was another time when she contracted a staph infection in her skull during one of many surgeries, forcing her to live for six months with part of her skull removed. Shelley's short-term memory would fail, due to having a small part of her brain removed as surgeons tried to curtail the deadly cancer's growth. Even through these trials, Shelley remained positive with her beaming smile lighting up from beneath the white baseball cap she often wore over her hairless head.

During the progression of Shelley's cancer, she was no longer able to work, at which time her life insurance policy's "waiver of premium" benefit took over her payments, allowing her policy to continue to grow, as if she had been making the premium payments herself all along. Instead, the insurance company was making those payments for her.

In addition, the underlying cash value inside her policy continued to grow, as well as the eventual death benefit. To me, the element of the additional paid-up insurance her policy was accumulating each year seemed almost magical. For each of those remaining years of Shelley's life, her future benefit for Kaitlyn was actually growing; and as each additional insurance amount was added to her policy, it was guaranteed for the future by the issuing insurance company.

-----

Besides my visit with Kaitlyn and her grandparents, Kathy and Bud, I also visited with Shelley's ex-husband, Jason. Life can be complicated, as it was with Shelley and Jason. During times of stress, marriages can sometimes fail, as did theirs. Kathy would tell me later that despite their difficulties Jason would find ways to give Shelley comfort through her final journey.

Kathy was focused on having as much of Shelley's care as possible take place in their home. Overlooking her own wellbeing, Kathy often complained that her clothes were becoming too baggy, not realizing that she had lost nearly sixty pounds while she looked after her ailing daughter.

Shelley's death wasn't quick. I remember visiting with her on several occasions. Throughout, her attitude was surprisingly upbeat. Her mother, Kathy, said, "Perhaps Shelley's short-term memory loss was a blessing."

Eventually, Shelley entered hospice and passed away. Kaitlyn, her daughter, was just ten years old.

-----

# Chapter Ten

After their divorce, the ownership of Shelley's life insurance policy was transferred to her mother, and the beneficiary of the policy became a trust set up for Kaitlyn's benefit. This trust allowed Kaitlyn to travel to France with her French class during high school, and it provided the means to attend school without the burden of college debt. It allowed her the start to a life that Shelley would have wanted to give her. Without even knowing who that little person was that growing inside her when we originally applied for life insurance, Shelley was doing the responsible thing that parents do: preparing for the known and the unknown.

It's sad when a family learns of the importance of life insurance, at the time the life insurance is actually needed. Shelley's parents were more than skeptical in the beginning. Had they talked her out of the decision she had made, the outcome would have been the same: death. But the life of Shelley's daughter would have been forever changed.

Kaitlyn told me when we visited, years after her mother's death, "I think I've had to grow up faster than others, who are my same age. In fact, many people believe that I'm older than I actually am. I remember a lot of my mom, just before she passed away, when I was younger. It was the summer between fourth and fifth grade.

"I miss my mom's smile, though people will tell me that my smile is the same as my mom's; so I sometimes feel that my mom is right here with me," Kaitlyn said. "I tend to think of others, before myself; and I believe my mother was the same way."

She was.

Investments Don't Hug

# Chapter Eleven

*Whole life: Built to last*

In our discussion of term insurance earlier, I referred to making premium payments as almost akin to making rent payments for an apartment. Using its most simplistic definition, the purchase of term insurance is made to provide coverage for a "term of time." It is not considered permanent. When a young couple invites friends and family to their apartment, they'll say, "Oh, we're just renting right now." But, when the same friends and family visit the house that couple has just acquired (with a mortgage), they refer to it as "the house we've bought," even though they're actually paying for it over a period of time, perhaps fifteen, twenty or thirty years. In their minds, the concept of homeownership implies permanence.

Permanent life insurance can come in many different varieties, as do houses, which may take on the styles of ranch, contemporary, Cape Cod, craftsman, cottage, or colonial. Just as HGTV has caused homeowners to seek out new and different designs for where and how they live, the competitiveness of insurance companies has caused the marketplace to become inundated with new and improved versions of contracts offering creative bells and whistles to attract new customers.

New updated versions of the solid traditional home which we'll call permanent life insurance arrive to the market place practically daily, though they are all required to go through the process of approval by the state insurance commissioner's office for each state in which the insurance company does business, in addition to registering the policies with the proper securities regulators, if that's a requirement of the product they may be offering to the public.

You may think of the process of manufacturing life insurance policies similar to following a "building code" for a general contractor. Each insurance company is required to follow established building standards. It doesn't necessarily mean one house is better than another or that one life insurance policy is better than another. They're different; but, if they're being offered to the public, they have to be "built to code."

For the purposes of this book, I'll discuss two divergent types of life insurance policies. Earlier we reviewed term insurance and how it serves to provide coverage for a term of time. Conversely, permanent life insurance is just that; it's considered to be a purchase that you may own for your whole life, hence its name: *whole life*. It may also be called *ordinary life* or *participating whole life*. This product is usually distributed through a mutual life insurance company or a mutual holding company.

Some life insurance companies will tout their policies as being permanent policies, but they might be pushing the envelope a little to make that claim. Let me just say because of the guarantees, "some permanent policies might be whole life, but all whole life policies are permanent." The guarantees established through whole life policies have existed for more than a century. Of course, these guarantees are subject to the claims paying ability of the life insurer that issues the policy.

Where term insurance is priced for a "term of time," whole life insurance is priced to last your entire lifetime. It's calculated in most situations to last or to "endow" at the age of 121. To endow means guaranteeing to pay out the entire death benefit amount if the insured is still alive at the age of 121. So, if someone has purchased a $1,000,000 whole life insurance policy, the insurance company would guarantee a payment of $1,000,000 at that age if the insured is still living; and obviously earlier, if the insured dies, less any policy loans which may have been taken against the policy.

Now, at this point you're probably chuckling under your breath, if not out loud, about the age of 121. This is actually a recent change to whole life policies as dictated by insurance regulations. Prior to the 2001 CSO (Commissioners Standard Ordinary) mortality tables, whole life insurance policies matured or endowed at the age of 100. This previous age requirement presented a problem that needed to be addressed.

If a benefit is received due to a person's death, it's generally free of income taxes. But, if a policy "endows" prior to the death of the insured, it becomes a taxable event. That's a problem; and the national association of state insurance commissioners realized a change needed to be made to life insurance contracts to protect those few individuals who would live beyond the age of 100 from dying of a heart attack when they received a notice from the IRS regarding the taxes due on their endowed policies.

In the late 1980s, when I began my career, people laughed at the thought of living to age 100, which was the endowment date prescribed by life insurance statutes at that time. Today, it's not a total surprise to know someone who has surpassed the centennial age, including my own grandmother on my mother's side, who lived to be one hundred years and two months.

The pricing of whole life policies are actuarially the same for every man, woman, boy, or girl, no matter their ages. An actuary is a professional who measures risk and uncertainty, and they are one of the most important elements in determining the price of all life insurance products. In theory, a parent who buys a life insurance policy on a newborn child has entered into a legal contract with a life insurance company requiring it to maintain the policy as long as the premiums are paid, at an established price, for the next 121 years. That's one heck of a commitment for the life insurance company to make for a modest annual premium.

Here's one way to visualize the pricing of a whole life insurance contract. Imagine a concertina, a musical instrument smaller than an accordion, but able to extend itself out farther from side to side, as the hands grasping each end are pulled apart from one another. When the musician extends his or her hands out the farthest from each other, that's representative of a newborn's policy, showing the greatest distance or in this example, the time period between birth and death (at age 121).

As the actuary makes calculations regarding the chances of death (i.e., mortality) the potential investment returns of the company and the administration costs of the policy, the concertina performer begins to squeeze the ends closer together. If the baby is a boy, already there is slightly less space left than if the baby is a girl, due to the long-term affects of mortality—females living longer than males. If the person is in their twenties it's squeezed some more, then again at thirty, forty, fifty, and sixty and so on. The actual price paid is the same total actuarial amount over time; it has simply been "squeezed" or adjusted due to the age of the individual, since they don't have the same amount of time in which to pay the premiums.

The initial price established at the start of the whole life policy, the issue date, is the same premium the insured will pay throughout the length of the "base" policy. The base refers to the standard "chassis" of a whole life policy, excluding any additional "riders" or add-ons that may have been included and could change the pricing over time. Some policies may have limited payment periods, some may provide for longer periods of payment. Neither type is necessarily better than the other; they are, in essence, actuarially equal. Each is just a different way of helping the insured accomplish specific goals.

The older the insured, the less time there is to pay the equivalent premiums. In addition, the concertina may be squeezed even more if the insured is a smoker, is overweight, is a diabetic, or has some other life-shortening ailment. The pricing is structured this way because when the policy eventually endows, the insurance company is required to pay out the guaranteed "face amount," that is the death benefit amount of the policy purchased, less any outstanding loans which may have been taken against the policy. In this way, the insurance company is treating everyone they insure equally and fairly. No one receives a "special deal."

A whole life policy may be a "participating" policy or a "non-participating" policy. A participating policy shares or "participates" in the profits of the insurance company. A non-participating policy does not participate in company profits.

A non-participating policy is pretty straight forward, as mentioned earlier. If you purchase a $1,000,000 life insurance policy on a newborn infant, and if that person is alive at the age 121, the holder of the policy will receive an endowment of $1,000,000. But, if you purchased a $1,000,000 participating policy on that child, there could be substantially more money that may accumulate over time, because of that policy's participation in the company's profits through the potential dividends it may have received.

Here's an analogy that might help. If I do business with a bank, which is owned by its shareholders, and I receive the services at a fair price, I'm satisfied. The bank made money, the shareholders made money, and I received the services I paid for. But, if I do business with a credit union, which is owned by its members (which include me), and I receive the services I need at a fair price, I'm satisfied and perhaps maybe a little bit more.

I received the services I paid for, the credit union made money, and as a member of the credit union I may have received an additional benefit by sharing in the profitability of my credit union. I am not saying a credit union is better than a bank or vice versa. They're just different from one another. Our own family has accounts at multiple financial institutions, including a credit union. We simply use different institutions for different purposes.

When owning a participating whole life insurance policy with a mutual structured life insurance company, as a policyholder you are actually considered a policy "owner." As the insurance company does better, you may do better as well. A participating policy allows you to share in the company's profits each year above what is required to be held for the company's reserves after the guaranteed cash values have been accounted for to each policy that they have in force. These profits are determined by the company's board of directors based on their mortality experience (i.e. fewer people died than they had budgeted for), administrative expenses, and the performance return of the company's investment portfolio.

In addition to managing risk, insurance companies are in the business of managing money and since they are responsible for providing for the needs of their policyholders, they have a due diligence to maintain adequate liquidity and a conservative portfolio, which typically consists of high-grade government and corporate bonds, commercial loans, and mortgages. An additional benefit of a mutual company structure is that the insurance company can take a long-term view of their company goals and investment approach, as opposed to a stock company which is constantly being followed by analysts focused on whether the next quarterly profitability projection will be met or not. This creates a constant pressure for returns from Wall Street. A mutual life insurance company does not have that same pressure. Again, one may not necessarily be better than the other. They are just different as to their corporate structure and approach to business.

Mutual life insurance companies reward their policyholders with these excess profits through the payment of dividends. Since there is no way of knowing what the profit of a company may be from year to year, dividends are not guaranteed; in my opinion, that's entirely okay. If the insurance company has experienced reduced earnings, then dividends may be reduced as well or not paid at all. On the other hand, as profitability increases, so should dividends. Many life insurance companies have been known to have consistently paid dividends for a hundred years or more. My own experience has shown that most company dividends change modestly from year to year, either up or down based on their long-term investments, mortality experience, and cost of doing business.

If you purchase a whole life policy, you might receive a declared dividend as early as the first anniversary of your life insurance policy, depending on the policy's design. It's more typical, though, to see dividends, if declared by the company's board of directors, beginning after the second or third year.

When a dividend is paid to the policy owner, it can usually be used in four different ways, though there are some additional variations depending on a company's product design. First, a dividend could be paid in cash (i.e. a check). When a typical whole life policy (which is not a MEC – Modified Endowment Contract – See Chapter 13: "A nearly perfect day") pays a dividend in cash, the payment is generally received tax-free, due to the concept of FIFO (First In, First Out). This is an accounting term. It means the dividend for tax purposes is considered analogous to a refund of the money you first put into the life insurance policy, which you had already paid taxes on. One reason not to choose this cash payment option is due to the fact that you would like your money and your policy to grow. Taking the dividend "seeds" away today means they won't be available in the future when you would like your "harvest" (the cash value and the death benefit) to be as large as possible.

A second option for which a dividend could be used is to reduce the out-of-pocket premiums that you are paying toward the purchase of your whole life insurance policy. This is an option I suggest holding off on until a later day. In the life insurance planning I have done for myself, I want my policies to grow and to have a larger death benefit and a larger equity of cash (cash value) in the future. Similar to taking a dividend in cash, this option chosen today might reduce the potential benefits that could be enjoyed in the future. Some may decide to use this option in retirement to reduce or possibly eliminate the ongoing outlay for life insurance premiums.

Many younger people would be surprised to learn that in my experience, at retirement many seniors love seeing the continued tax-deferred growth of their money and the increasing death benefit at a time when they may no longer be able to qualify for life insurance, due to declining health. It is a time when they may no longer make contributions into tax-deferred retirement accounts, such as IRAs. So, many seniors, if the insurance company allows, will continue to pay premiums to enable the continued growth of the cash values of their whole life insurance policies in addition to having an increasing death benefit.

A third option for using declared dividends is to leave the dividend with the policy to earn a competitive interest rate. These rates may be changed from time to time by the insurance company, depending upon current market conditions. But, there is typically a floor, or guaranteed lowest percentage rate, written into the contract that is often quite competitive. This might seem an attractive option, with one caveat. Though the dividend may be income tax-free, the interest earned on that dividend would be reportable each year on your tax return. I don't like taxes, so I have never recommended this option.

The fourth and best option, in my professional opinion, is to use the dividend to purchase additional paid-up insurance. Wait, wait, wait—before you stop reading, stay with me on this one. Most husbands especially, will say, "I don't want any more insurance!" Hey, I get that, but hear me out. Let's go over the mantra everyone has heard (or said) about why they don't like life insurance: It's because "you're worth more" ... What's the rest? ... That's right: "dead, than alive." That one statement is all you need to know to understand why this can be such a great asset to own.

Let me walk you through this dividend transaction. Let's say your annual dividend is going to be $250, because it's a rather young policy. Let's also say that this $250 would purchase $1,000 of additional paid-up life insurance. What's actually happened here? You just bought $1,000 of additional life insurance with an equity or cash value of $250. Your spouse is going to love that! But wait, it's "paid-up" additional life insurance, so you don't have to pay for it again, next year. It's yours forever! Also, it has been added to your original life insurance policy to increase its total value.

Let's continue, the $250 doesn't disappear with the purchase of the additional paid-up insurance. It's still there, too; and at anytime in the future, if you want that $250 in your pocket, all you need to do is to surrender the $1,000 of paid-up additional life insurance that was purchased. But, the value doesn't stop there.

Since the underlying $250 has a value, it also qualifies to earn its own dividend whenever the life insurance company declares dividends in the future. And here's my favorite part. There is no 1099 form showing that gain so you don't have to share that information with the IRS. It's like getting interest on your interest, but the values were cloaked inside your dividends and additional paid-up life insurance! So, you made money. Your spouse loves that you own more life insurance, and you both love not having to report it on your tax return. Cool, eh?

Oh, one more thing about dividends. Though dividends are not contractually guaranteed in the future, once declared by the life insurance company's board of directors and paid into your policy, those dividends are now fully guaranteed by the life insurance company, eliminating the risk of future loss. I call that great!

# Chapter Twelve

*"May I take your picture?"*

Holding an eight-by-ten inch framed graduation photo of her son, Beau, Mary looked straight ahead, into the lens of my camera that day in the office, with her big contagious smile captured permanently on film. I snapped the picture and said, "Now, you're only forty; but someday when you're old and grey you can look back at this and remember why you bought this life insurance policy."

Like many families, Mary's was a blended family consisting of her son, a husband, and his two children from a previous marriage, whom she had raised as her own.

As I relived that day, some years had passed since Mary's death. Her husband, Kirk, was pouring a second cup of coffee as we visited at his northern Wisconsin lake home. Fresh snow covered the landscape on that January day, as the sun tried to peek through an occasional opening in the clouds. Enough time had past that the hurt of his loss had lessened and we could sit, visit, and laugh about the good memories made during their thirty-year marriage.

Before they met, Kirk was running a Montgomery Ward store selling mostly appliances in the same rural community where Mary had been raised along with her six brothers and sisters. "Her mom was a die-hard Ward's shopper," Kirk told me, "So, I saw a lot of her."

Kirk knew the three sisters, but had never met Mary. She had been married for a short time, had a son and then soon divorced. Likewise, Kirk was also divorced and had two young children of his own.

Kirk called Mary's mother "Ma Baier," since her last name was pronounced the same as the three hundred pound animals that roam through parts of Wisconsin making sure their baby cubs are always safe. "So, Ma Baier came into the store one day," Kirk continued, "and she proclaimed 'Boy, do I have the girl for you.' Every time she came into the store, she would remind me that I didn't even need to date anyone else."

Ma Baier's thirtieth wedding anniversary with her husband, Jack, was coming up soon. Mary's mom came into the store to tell Kirk, "We're going to have a dance, and I want you to come up to the golf club and meet Mary. Remember, she's the one for you!"

Feeling like he had his dating life already under control, Kirk nonetheless relented. On that predestined night, he ran out to the golf club to keep his promise to Ma Baier.

When he arrived, it was as if he heard a murmur go through the room from Mary's sisters, "He's here." Though he danced with Mary's mother, he wasn't yet introduced to Mary, but instead only waved to her from across the room. As he was preparing to leave, one of Mary's sisters pull him aside saying the group was headed to a popular local tavern.

By the time Kirk arrived, Mary was already there. He practically laughed out loud while describing the plum colored dress Mary was wearing and how the remaining sunlight of the day was shining through a window creating an aura of light encircling her, when he entered the room. Suddenly, everyone became quiet again and there was another whisper of "He's here."

Kirk continued on with the story that he felt as if he were Moses, as the crowd seemed to part like the Red Sea. By now, Mary's mother led Kirk by the arm to introduce the two. He and Mary shared some small talk and helping to strike a small fire of their own, Mary's sister-in-law invited Kirk to join everyone for a small bonfire later that night at an area park.

Kirk said that he couldn't remember what he and Mary visited about during that evening bonfire, as the twinkle of the stars illuminated the night sky overhead, but they continued talking until the sunrise crested over the horizon.

Two years later they were married. Mary's son, Beau, was six. Kirk's son was also six, and his daughter was eight.

-----

I actually met Kirk and Mary when my wife, Betty, and I moved into the house next door to theirs. They had moved to town due to a job change for Kirk. We saw their children grow up and even had their daughter babysit for us on numerous occasions when our children were young. Mary also requested us to secretly keep a watchful eye from our house on "the boys" during their teenage years, whenever she and Kirk were away from home. The unspoken arrangement was that they were to do the same when our children were in their teens. But, after their children graduated from high school, they moved to a house in the next town over.

When I think of Mary, I remember a woman who was never self-conscious. She often worked a shift that allowed her to be home for part of the day. A wooded canopy of trees shaded their backyard, and Mary liked sporting a tan. So, it never surprised me when coming home for a quick lunch to spot Mary lying out in a bikini catching rays in the middle of their front yard as the traffic passed by.

Even though theirs was a blended family, they treated each of their children equally. Yet, Mary came to me with concerns at the age of forty that she wanted to discuss her own estate planning or more specifically, legacy planning for her son Beau.

Because of family trusts and the financial success through Kirk's extended family, Mary wanted to insure that her son would have some of the same future opportunities for himself that his step-brother and step-sister would probably be receiving from their side of the family.

We discussed several options. Mary wanted to be able to put money away on a regular basis, which could grow, but without the risk that it could be lost. She also liked the idea of the creation of an immediate estate. That's where life insurance shines. Upon approval of her application from the issuing insurance company and one month's premium paid, a legacy was instantly created.

As we continued to review Mary's policy each year, the time came when she decided she could add to her portfolio. The first policy was building equity (i.e. cash value) and had already paid two annual dividends, which added to her cash position. More importantly, it increased the policy's death benefit toward her legacy, something that term insurance policies don't do. So, at the age of forty-three Mary decided to double her life insurance coverage with an additional policy, as we went through the approval process once again.

We continued to meet annually to review and monitor the progress of her policies and visit about the changes in her life. In addition, I assisted Mary with some retirement accounts she owned.

When I first met Mary, she worked at the local brewery in the production department. Later she took on an opportunity as a travel agent, but her true calling came when she became an educational aide with a local school district. Her students were known as "Mary's kids." She loved that job.

About a decade after she purchased her second policy, some medical problems surfaced which required a hysterectomy.

Kirk remembers how Mary would sometimes get premonitions through her life, especially regarding her health. On the day prior to her surgery, she said it would be best for the doctors to also remove her ovaries, which wasn't part of the original plan. After the procedure, biopsies were completed, and it was thought an ovarian cancer was found, which would not have been discovered without the extraction of her ovaries, since the cancer was in the very early stages.

-----

When Mary was one month away from her fifty-fourth birthday, our office completed a claim form to place her two life insurance policies on "waiver of premium" benefit, due to disability. Because she had elected this important additional coverage at the time she applied for her life insurance, upon receiving the proper documentation and approval of the insurance company, the premiums on Mary's policies would be waived, having the company pay the premiums, continuing all the benefits without any further cost to her. Her policies continued to accumulate cash values, and each year, when a dividend was paid, Mary accrued additional paid-up insurance to build her legacy.

The cancer inside Mary had turned out to be peritoneal cancer, which develops in the thin layer of tissue that lines the abdomen. Though in pain, Mary continued with her upbeat attitude. Her body, however, eventually tired, and Mary died at the age of fifty-five.

Every death is difficult. When the person has lived a considerably long life you can focus on the celebration of that life lived, but when it's shortened like Mary's, it seems there are so many empty holes left. Yet, we always come together as family and friends to celebrate the life by which we have been touched. As Betty and I hugged each of the family members after the church service that Thursday evening, I searched for the words I would share with Beau. I don't remember what I said, but I remember thinking to myself that I was thankful Mary and I had done the right thing in planning her legacy.

Later, Beau and I had a chance to visit about Mary's legacy planning. He knew his mom had done some planning with me, but he wasn't quite sure what it was. I showed him a copy of that photo which I took of his mother when she began her legacy planning just fifteen years earlier. There she was young and healthy with her contagious smile captured permanently on film, all while proudly holding that eight-by-ten inch framed graduation photo of her son.

What did Beau do with Mary's legacy plan? I know he was able to move his growing family from a small ranch style house to a home where they wouldn't be squeezed for space. My guess, if he's like most young parents his age, he probably had some bills to pay off and perhaps found himself with less stress in his life because of some simple planning that his mother had carried out as her legacy for him.

When Mary and Kirk discussed their own money, it was agreed that they would leave their share to one another, and that upon the last death their estate would be divided equally among all the children. But Mary was concerned that her son, Beau, may not receive the same potential legacy that could be inherited by his siblings in the future from her husband's extended family. Life insurance legacy planning is the way she created predetermined wealth to pass on to Beau.

Life insurance can become the great equalizer.

Could Mary have used investments to create this bequest? Yes, but not with the certainty that she wanted. According to the Social Security Administration's actuarial life tables, at the age of forty, when her first policy was purchased, an average woman should have lived for an additional forty-two years. She wasn't quite at the midway point of her expected life. Based on that, wouldn't the stock market seem to be a better gamble?

Some would have you believe that an expected outcome can be projected by using an average rate of return on an investment. But that simply doesn't always work. Let's take this example that I often share with new clients.

Imagine you have found the perfect investment. In year one, you have a 15 percent return. In year two, you have a 15 percent return. Then in year three, you take a 15 percent loss. How much of a gain would you need to receive in year number four, just to get back to your average 15 percent annualized rate of return?

No one has ever guessed the correct answer. It's 56 percent! That's the return you would need to get in year number four to bring your average return back to 15 percent, and I don't think the odds are in your favor of that ever happening.

-----

Mary also understood the concept of building a life insurance portfolio. Over time, I have personally added additional policies on my own life, building one upon another. It would be unusual for most people to only own one stock, one mutual fund or one certificate of deposit. When it comes to investments we understand the theory of portfolio building. Some agents may try to convince potential clients to consolidate older policies into a new and improved policy. Unfortunately, that may not necessarily be the appropriate strategy to use.

When Mary purchased her first life insurance policy at the age of forty, the contractual terms and pricing were based on a forty-year-old woman. Likewise, three years later, when an additional policy was added to her portfolio at the age of forty-three, the pricing structure was based upon what I like to call (with a smirk), a new and improved age.

Oh, one last thing. When Beau and I discussed Mary's legacy after his mom's death, he asked a question that I sometimes forget to address, simply because I deal with this all the time and regular folks don't. Here's the question he asked: "How much tax am I going to have to pay on this?" "None", I replied. "When done right, and your mother did it right, there are no income taxes to pay." He was stunned.

Mary had created a probate-free, risk-free, and income tax-free legacy by embracing the life insurance asset.

Investments Don't Hug

# Chapter Thirteen

*"A nearly perfect day"*

Connie shared with me that for her and her husband, Cotter, to spend an entire day together from eight o'clock in the morning until the sun ended its journey across the sky and disappeared over the horizon, only happened perhaps three times throughout their entire thirty-nine year marriage. Cotter, whose given name was Carl, always needed to be on the move, viewing moments of idleness as a waste of time. Feverishly, he was always going over lists of projects that needed to be completed. Even during those moments between a job for others and a project for his family, Cotter's relaxation meant going out into the woods alone, cutting down trees and, if the fallen trunks weren't too large, finishing the lumbering by splitting the logs by hand with an axe and maul.

Cotter was a carpenter by trade, but prided himself in being a handyman of sorts, not shy at all to attack projects of nearly any size. He built the house he and Connie called home, living in it for a year before they married. He literally constructed it from the ground up, beginning the project with a $10,000 loan. He never liked borrowing money, but the loan allowed him to build a simple basement home below ground level with a roof overhead. That's where he and Connie would begin their lives together, living in a simple basement home for their first two years as husband and wife. As Cotter could afford more lumber, he would build walls for the future ground floor addition, piece by piece in his father's empty hay barn. As he added those walls to their basement home, it created a modest twenty-eight by forty foot ranch style house, where he and Connie would bring up their two sons.

As Connie walked through the house after Cotter's death, touching the walls and trim work, everywhere she looked, she would see Cotter. "Every piece of woodwork," she said, "was Cotter."

-----

I don't recall the conversation we had when I first met Connie a decade earlier. Having been invited to speak at a regional military base nearby, we probably exchanged some simple pleasantries as I worked my way through the dining hall introducing myself prior to giving a short talk at a noon hour luncheon about retirement preparation to about twenty civil service employees.

What I didn't know is that over the next several years Connie would pester Cotter saying, "We need to look at what we've got. We've got money lying in savings and it's just not doing anything for us. Let's just go talk to somebody and see what we can do. It doesn't have to be high risk."

"I know that was one of the things I said to him," she would tell me later. "But, he would simply answer back with a 'well,' and would then just grumble under his breath."

"Do you remember when we came to your office for the very first time?" Connie asked me. Actually, I did. Connie was talkative and Cotter, wearing his baseball cap covering his bald head that seldom saw the light of the sun, was quiet, though he occasionally spoke up, just to let me know he was the boss. I would chuckle to myself, thinking "But, it was Connie who got you here."

Connie echoed the past when she reminded me years later, "Mark, he didn't want to tell you anything." Continuing, she repeated that she would pester him regularly, that this meeting with me was what she wanted to do. Trying to make a case for their very first visit with me, Connie would try to say again convincingly, "I believe we can invest without being high risk." But, with Cotter, she remembered he would merely bark back "If I have $10,000, I want my $10,000 in my hands, not someone else's."

That's why their house went up so slowly. "If I'm going to have a house, I'm going to build it with my own money. I'm not going to go to a bank and get a loan. I'm going to do it with my own money," he would say. Thriftiness carried on elsewhere in Cotter's life too. He never purchased a car with a loan. "He would rather walk," said Connie, "than get a loan for a car."

I asked Connie, "What was the most difficult thing for Cotter to wrap his mind around during our visits together, do you suppose: the life insurance or the investments?"

"The investments," she replied. "Life insurance was easy, because he already believed in its value, though he didn't in the beginning years, when we were younger."

-----

Years earlier, an agent came to their home and sold them a life insurance policy. What made Cotter understand the importance of how life insurance worked is when the agent asked Cotter, "If you died tomorrow, what would happen to your two young boys?"

Connie was independent and strong herself, and Cotter felt that she could manage on her own, but he was worried and concerned about how Connie would make it with two young boys at home with his income no longer coming into the house; and he also had the same worries for himself, if Connie were to die prematurely.

"But, that was life insurance from back then, when the two of you had youngsters at home," I reminded Connie. "Your kids have been out of the house for years. Why did he buy the additional life insurance when we worked together?"

"Cotter realized," she said, "that he didn't have to die to get at his money, because if we needed that money we could get our hands on it. It was liquid and available, if something happened. In addition, after the first several years we had more money available to us building inside our new polices if we needed it, than what we had originally paid into them. Plus, with the additional life insurance policies, we didn't have to report our increasing cash values that grew inside the policies on our tax returns.

Had we kept that money in the bank instead, the money we would have earned would have been reported on our tax returns."

-----

When most people obtain life insurance, the purchase is usually made with a series of payments similar to a mortgage payment. Policies are typically purchased through monthly premiums, though they could sometimes be paid annually, semi-annually or quarterly. But, a life insurance policy can also be purchased with one single lump-sum payment or premium, in this case with a single premium whole life policy. In fact, the single premium policies were structured for Cotter and Connie in such a way that any additional premium payments would not have even been allowed. Cotter loved that. He didn't like anything that looked or smelled like an ongoing bill.

Based on the contractual guarantees of their policies, the initial death benefits they acquired were nearly double the single one-time premium they had paid; and it happened immediately. In addition, the guaranteed surrender values of their contracts, had they changed their minds within the first few years, could have been returned to them by simply cashing out (i.e., surrendering) the policies, giving them more than what their initial premium had been.

Adding a life insurance portfolio as an alternative to their bank certificates of deposit met their goals of liquidity, plus tax-deferred growth with a probate-free and income-tax-free death benefit substantially larger than what their initial premium had been; their decision to move ahead became a no brainer.

Since whole life policies often mirror the long-term rates of return of highly-rated bond portfolios, they don't experience the day-to-day volatility experienced with many traditional market-driven investments. Plus, they also have the safety of having the values guaranteed by the issuing life insurance company. "I always told my boys," said Connie, "if something catastrophic happens, we'll be taken care of."

In addition to developing a portfolio of life insurance policies, Connie appreciated the modest investment portfolio we created together. Other than a retirement plan through Connie's employer, she and Cotter had never really invested in equity products before. But, it was the life insurance with its guarantees that gave Cotter the most comfort. It provided some comfort to Connie, as well, because of the unknown future we all experience during our lifetimes.

-----

As bullheaded as he was about other things, Cotter was good about going to the doctor. When we first met at my office, Cotter was fifty-eight years old. "He had just had a physical in September and everything came back good, the blood work-up and all," Connie remarked. But, then the nearly perfect day happened.

"We spent the whole day together, the entire day," Connie reminisced. "We took a leisurely drive to visit my brother. Cotter hadn't done anything strenuous all day. He wasn't in the woods, as he enjoyed doing; which is what he was actually planning on doing that day. He had also planned on doing a bathroom plumbing project, but he couldn't reach the fellow to do the job. So, he asked me, 'You want to go for a ride or do something.' Seldom did that ever happen, because he was always busy."

"The guy did not sit still," Connie said, "and for us to be together for a whole day, that was very unusual. He would always be off doing something. So, for us to spend the entire day together, I think it was meant to be."

"My brother had talked about buying a cabin up north." Connie said. "So, Cotter suggested that we go and see what they were doing about that cabin. I remember Cotter saying to my brother Brian, "I think it needs a lot of work,' and then Cotter said, 'just give me the keys.' That was just like Cotter. He continued by saying, 'Whatever you need done, I'll drive up and do it.'"

"Afterward, we went to a casino for about an hour. I was up, but Cotter lost his $20. That was his self-imposed limit," Connie said with a laugh. "So, we were only there for about an hour. We stopped and had lunch and then went back to visit with my brother again. Afterward, we came home. We must have gotten home around six or seven o'clock. We were outside around eight-thirty watching some storms pass by. We just stood outside watching the storms come in. It wasn't raining, but the skies were ominous."

She remembers that heat lighting from the distant thunderstorms filled the sky with faint flashes on the horizon. "We were enjoying the show that nature was putting on for us," she said. "At about nine o'clock we came back into the house, Cotter entered first and walked down the hallway, while I turned and shut the door. And that's when I heard the loud thud."

It was a sound that still makes Connie pause today, whenever she remembers it. The sound was Cotter falling.

"I can still remember saying 'Cotter, what the hell are you doing?' thinking he had simply slipped. The minute I got to him, I knew; and when my son Neil got to the house, shortly after the ambulance had arrived, he knew too, that his dad was gone." Cotter was only sixty-five.

-----

It was October. Just a month before, Cotter had passed his annual physical with flying colors. "It's funny," said Connie. "What really meant a lot to me was that Cotter's doctor contacted me that Friday morning and said 'I'm just calling to tell you how sorry I am. I went back through his records and I don't think I missed anything.'"

"I believe 'your day' is marked," Connie expressed to me. "I do believe that. I believe the day you are born, the day of your death has already been determined."

Cotter didn't want a funeral. That would not have been his style. Instead, there would be a memorial service at a local community center. I think the family thought it was going to be a small gathering, but as I drove through the sunny countryside to the small unincorporated village along the single lane state highway, the line of mourners coming to pay their respects already extended outside and around the corner of the building. After I took my place in the procession of friends, it would still be a couple of hours before the line would make its way inside the building and down the hallway to where the family gathered together.

Cotter would have wanted a celebration, and he got it. As I wound through the community center, I couldn't help smiling as I saw the old black and white photos of the dashing young man with a full head of hair followed by the additional pictures that told stories from the chapters of his life with Connie: marriage, kids, grandchildren, and photos of Cotter enjoying ocean beaches, something we don't have in the upper Midwest. "He loved the ocean," Connie would tell me later. I had the opportunity to meet their fine sons, and when I worked my way up through the line to Connie, we embraced. "I didn't expect to see you," she said. "I'm not here on business," I replied. "I'm here for a friend".

-----

None of us know how life will play out. The best planning in the world cannot take into account all the variables. Helping to prepare for all possible outcomes requires planning for the best, while preparing ourselves for the worse. That's why we click our seatbelts before turning the ignitions in our cars. When our own children were young, my wife, Betty, actually convinced our children that the car wouldn't start unless all the seatbelts were fastened. Testing her statement once, Betty remembers demanding from the reflection in the rearview mirror to our children in the backseat, "Who doesn't have their seatbelt fastened, the car won't start?" Then one of the kids sheepishly clicked their belt together.

Cotter wanted safety and liquidity. He would have worded it slightly differently—I want a guarantee, and when I want my money, I want to get at it. The single premium life insurance policies he and Connie purchased provided an appropriate complement to their otherwise moderately conservative investments. The additional death benefit provided through their life insurances also provided security. Cotter wanted everything to run smoothly under his terms, not someone else's. The life insurance policies he and Connie purchased provided just that—steady guaranteed growth and the opportunity for additional growth through the potential dividends that could be declared by the issuing life insurance company. Those dividends increased his death benefit. His life insurance asset also grew tax-deferred and it became income tax-free at exactly the time it was needed, at his death. After our office received Cotter's death certificate, Connie received the benefit the two of them seldom talked about, but which was set in place seven years earlier, as a promise to each other through a simple contract issued through a life insurance company.

After Cotter's death, Connie and I sat in my office and talked for a long time. We didn't talk about money, because in the end, as stubborn as he was, Cotter had done the right thing and now money wouldn't be a problem. Instead, we enjoyed our time visiting about Cotter and their life together, at moments our conversation was very serious and quiet; and then in an instant we would find ourselves laughing as Connie shared stories of their long marriage together.

Connie would declare: "I'm mad at him. We were supposed to be together into our eighties, still arguing about what movies to watch," and then with a smile, added, "You really had to know Cotter to love him."

For myself, I still smile to this day when I think of Cotter leaving my office with a devilish grin on his face that I always interpreted as saying, "Remember, I'm the boss."

-----

It's too bad that most financial advisors spend so much of their time trying each day to manage the risk of a client's portfolio, seeking out a client's tolerance for market volatility. What they really do in the end is to try and manage a client's expectations. When the market is high, they chime in, "Don't get too excited, this probably won't continue." Then when the market is low, they encourage, "Don't get too excited, this probably won't continue." All the advisor seems to do sometimes is to change the inflection in their voice from positive to that of concern using the same words. When permanent whole life insurance is used, the conversation of risk doesn't need to happen, since it's a place for a client's safe money.

It's difficult to convince someone in their mid-sixties to think long-term. It's not necessarily correct to have all of a person's assets "invested." Cotter's closest brush with risk might have been the $20 that he was willing to lose at a casino. But, he probably entered the building thinking to himself, "How long can I make this $20 last?" He had already decided ahead of time what his limit was for the afternoon of entertainment. But, for his real assets, it was a completely different story. I think he invested in the lower risk mutual funds due to Connie's insistence. But, the life insurance policies provided the certainty he and Connie wanted.

In Chapter Fourteen we will discuss the cash value and payment structures of whole life insurance policies. Like a mortgage, this type of policy may be purchased over time or, in the case of Cotter and Connie, it could be purchased with one lump sum premium payment, as some might purchase a house with a single cash payment. Here's how a single premium whole life insurance policy works:

- There's one single premium payment. That's it!
- It provides for a guaranteed level death benefit.
- The policy stipulates a guaranteed predetermined table of future cash surrender values, based on the initial premium paid.
- The contract provides liquidity, though slightly less than the initial premium if the policy were to be surrendered in the first several years. (Sorry, even banks advertise "Substantial penalties for early withdrawal.")
- Tax-deferred growth. As the policy grows, the insurance company won't issue a 1099 for your tax return, unless you surrender your policy and then you will only be taxed for the amount in excess of the initial premium paid. This is opposite of a bank certificate of deposit. At the end of each year with a bank CD, even if you didn't take any money out of the certificate, the earned interest is still reportable to the IRS.
- There's the potential for even greater growth. A mutual insurance company may declare dividends. By doing so, this would be additional money that could be added to your policy to accentuate its growth, tax-deferred. If you were to decide to receive a declared dividend in cash, as opposed to

leaving it inside the policy, that dividend would be taxable (See the discussion of MECs below).

- When dividends are paid, there is the potential for an increased death benefit. If the mutual insurance company declares dividends, this extra money may be used to purchase additional paid-up insurance increasing the policy's death benefit potential, in addition to increasing the underlining value of money growing tax-deferred into the policy.

There is one additional caveat to a single premium whole life insurance policy that should be noted. Since the entire premium is being paid at one time, it changes the treatment of the policy's cash value from FIFO (First In, First Out) to LIFO (Last In, First Out). This means that any money coming out of the policy first (i.e. any gain) is taxable. So, in that respect the life insurance policy acts similar to any other annuity or investment product. For tax purposes, a single premium whole life insurance policy is considered a MEC (Modified Endowment Contract). In addition, it also means that if the contract is surrendered for its cash value prior to the age of 59 ½ there is an additional 10 percent tax penalty due on any gain in the policy's cash value. In that way, it would be similar to other retirement accounts, such as a traditional IRA or 401(k) that have the same penalty structure.

But here's the thing. Unlike a traditional IRA or 401(k), at death, regardless of age, the death benefit of a single premium whole life insurance policy is generally received income tax-free. It's been my experience that a whole life product of this type, by and large, is best suited for clients from their mid-fifties and older who want to accumulate money in a safe place that will grow conservatively with guaranteed values, with the potential for additional growth—all of which can grow tax-deferred, while providing liquidity. Yet, at the end of the day when death occurs it may still provide an income tax-free death benefit and, if the proper beneficiary documentation is completed, it can also be free of probate.

# Chapter Fourteen

*Understanding cash values*

We covered quite a bit of territory about the basics of whole life insurance in Chapter Eleven. To recap:

- Whole life insurance lasts your whole life or at least until the age of 121.
- The guaranteed cash inside your policy equals the death benefit at age 121.
- Dividends, as declared by the insurance company may enhance the cash growing inside your policy, as well as increasing the total death benefit.

Why would you want to own life insurance for the rest of your life? Isn't the idea to protect your family against a hardship until you've accumulated enough money that you wouldn't need to have life insurance? That's a great question! This will be addressed in Chapter Sixteen, "What's left?" But for now, let's delve a little deeper into how this product actually works and, more specifically, how the cash values of a whole life insurance policy work.

To continue the discussion, let's build upon the example of owning a home, which was used in Chapter Five, "Human Life Value."

Let's assume you were able to purchase a home with no money down and you acquired a fixed-rate thirty-year mortgage. This design could look a lot like the structure of a whole life insurance policy. The mortgage payment could represent your ongoing premium payment. It's a contractually fixed amount of money. The initial value of the house would represent the "face amount" or death benefit of the policy and the accumulated equity of the home could represent the guaranteed cash value inside the whole life policy.

When the mortgage is satisfied, the equity inside the home equals the value of the home. Let's go one step farther. Since your home is expected to increase in value over time, we'll include the anticipated dividends in addition to the annual increases in guaranteed cash value with this illustration. This increased value represented by dividends the insurance company may declare would enhance the future value of your whole life insurance policy by increasing both the equity or cash value portion of the policy and the ultimate death benefit.

As a homeowner, after a full year of making twelve monthly mortgage payments, how much of your house do you actually own? If you look at the amortization schedule provided by your mortgage lender, you might be lucky if you own a single doorknob. What about after year number two? Now, you might actually own a door. After three years, you might own the doorframe holding the door to the wall. Wow! Wasn't this a great idea to buy a house?

Yes, it was. Because you understand something that your parents knew and your grandparents knew. That this purchase of a house could become the single largest asset of your lifetime, but it builds slowly, year after year, over time. It doesn't create value immediately overnight.

If you understand the equity build-up inside your home, you now understand the trajectory of the guaranteed values of a whole life insurance policy. It's akin to a house. After the first year, your policy may have little or no cash value depending on its design. But, remember the life insurance company has taken on the risk of potentially paying a huge death claim immediately after the first premium payment was paid and they have also promised to structure your policy to last a lifetime. After the second year, more cash is accumulating inside your policy and after the third year, even more.

Our example with a home mortgage thus far, assumes a no-money down approach; but perhaps you want to build greater equity in your home right away. Then you typically would put a ten, fifteen or twenty percent down payment toward your home purchase immediately. You can also do that with a whole life insurance policy too, which would immediately begin building "equity" or cash value inside your policy faster. But unlike a home that doesn't increase in value when you put a down payment towards a mortgage, a down payment or a "single payment paid-up additions rider" immediately increases the policy's death benefit, in addition to the policy's cash value. Plus, this initial "down payment" is eligible for dividends as early as the first anniversary of the whole life insurance policy!

Some homeowners would like to shorten the amount of time they have to pay an ongoing mortgage payment. So, they might decide to prepay their mortgage ahead by adding an additional amount of money to their payment each month. You can do the very same thing with a whole life insurance policy; for this, the insurance company uses a generic term of an "annual paid-up additions rider" payment. Again, this extra amount paid into your policy immediately increases your policy's death benefit, in addition to its cash value. Plus, this extra amount paid is also eligible for dividends as the insurance company declares them.

Here's the big difference in our mortgage/house analogy. When making a mortgage payment toward a home, each payment represents one part that goes to the principle repayment of the loan and one part that goes towards the interest cost of that loan. If you have a thirty-year mortgage, which represents three hundred sixty monthly mortgage payments, at what point within that amortization schedule is one hundred percent of your payment going toward the principle with nothing going toward the interest payment? This isn't a trick question. The answer is never. Even though that final three-hundred-sixtieth payment is mostly principal, there's still a little bit of interest remaining even on that very last payment. So, there is never a time when you see the amount of your payment being equal to the gain of the equity inside your house.

Not all whole life policies are as simple as our example above. Depending upon the specific design of the policy, the annual guaranteed cash value increases combined with the declared annual dividend inside a whole life insurance policy may actually equal or surpass the annual premium paid within the first four to five years of a whole life insurance policy. Now, your life insurance policy is looking better than your house purchase!

Similar to your home, a whole life insurance policy also has the ability to be used for loans in the event you need some ready cash. Views differ somewhat on this subject. If you want to take the family to Disney World, you should be saving extra money someplace else for your vacations. I believe the cash value inside a whole life insurance policy should only be used for significant life-changing events or opportunities.

For example, my wife Betty and I have creatively used our life insurance portfolio as a catalyst to purchase investment real estate. We've accessed money through the use of policy loans. When our commercial lender asked if the bank could erect a sign in front of our commercial building when Betty was acting as the general contractor for a major building remodeling project, I thought to myself, maybe I should have put a sign up of my own saying "This project is partially funded through a loan taken against Mark Bertrang's whole life insurance policy."

I also used a policy loan during the initial year of the Great Recession to fund some business improvements during a year when regular revenue couldn't generate the income needed to move ahead with the plans I knew would pay off in the long-term.

Once, a client who is an avid sportsman called my office and explained how he had an opportunity to buy forty acres of hunting land, but he had no idea how he was going to do it, since he didn't have the amount of money he needed and the vast majority of his assets were locked inside a state pension fund. I asked if I could check some numbers and get back to him. After hanging up the phone, I pulled his whole life insurance policy information up on my computer and ran through some financial calculations before calling him back a few short minutes later.

When he answered, I asked, "Can you make a $75 a month payment?" "Sure," he laughed. "Go buy the land," I said.

I then took the next fifteen minutes explaining how a loan against his life insurance policy would cover what he needed for the land and how the monthly $75 would be the cost over time to repay the money from his policy loan. He never realized his whole life insurance could be used in that way. He now enjoys hunting with his sons on their own land.

Now an uneducated insurance client might ask, "Why would I have to take a loan out from my policy to use my own money?" Let's go back to our home ownership example.

If I decide in the future to take out a home equity loan against my house, I have to go to the bank, apply for the loan, and pay whatever fees the bank requires me to pay. The bank will run a credit check on me to find out what my FICO score is; they may also need to have an appraisal done on my house. Then if I qualify and I'm approved, they'll determine the rate of interest I'll pay, based on my credit worthiness, and commit me to a fixed payment schedule to be paid on time, so I won't default and lose my house which I have now put at risk, as collateral. What a fun process that is, right?

Here's the process for taking out a loan against a whole life insurance policy. Knowing the loan amount available inside your life insurance, while taking a shower one morning you decide that you need some of the money. After drying off, you call your insurance agent to fill the forms out for you. That morning you drop by the agent's office to provide a signature. It's faxed to the home office and a check is in the mail to your home within the next few days. Which example sounds easier to you—the bank or the insurance company?

Unlike getting money from your house, you didn't have to ask a lender to get at your own money. In addition, the payback schedule is going to be determined by you. Since you want the money returned as soon as you can, so you can use it again, it's your choice if it's paid back in a few months, a few years, or a few decades. You're the policy owner. It's your choice. The interest rate you'll pay for the loan will be determined by the terms of the policy. Usually, the interest rate is based on a specifically published long-term bond rate. But, you're still asking why do you have to pay interest to get at your own money? The short answer is that the loan you receive isn't your money.

Let's return to the home example once more. When you take out a home equity loan through a lender, the money you receive is "their" money. The value of the loan is determined by the equity inside your home. You never receive the money from your home. It's still in your house. Your home is acting as collateral for your loan.

Likewise with your policy loan; the money you receive through your policy is the insurance company's money. Guess what? Your money is still inside your policy, doing all the wonderful things it was doing before your loan was taken. Your policy is simply being used as collateral for the money the life insurance company has sent you in the form of a loan.

Let's go one more step. If you were to sell your house at this point, how much money would you receive? You would receive whatever your home equity is minus your outstanding loan. It works the same way with your life insurance, if the contract is surrendered at this point, you would receive whatever the cash value is, minus any outstanding loan. Likewise, if you were to die at this point, the life insurance company would pay out a death benefit minus the outstanding loan amount.

Over the years, I have had the opportunity to address many investment and insurance organizations. I am continually surprised at how many financial professionals don't understand what has just been explained to you, in a few short paragraphs. Just because someone has a license to sell insurance doesn't mean they totally understand how it works.

You can typically figure out immediately if an agent understands how whole life policy loans work. If the agent uses the word "from," as in "you can borrow 'from' your policy," they don't understand how policy loans work. But if the agent uses the word "against," as in "you may borrow 'against' your policy," this agent probably understands these policy loan concepts.

Each year, I buy a fishing license and each year I am humbled that I'm not very good at catching fish. Unfortunately, a license doesn't mean a thorough knowledge of insurance products. It usually only means that the person has been taught how to do things "legally," similar to the fishing regulations book I receive each year that tells me the maximum limits of fish that I can take in a single day, as if that's ever been my problem. Later, I will share more information on what to look for in a life insurance agent.

Besides whole life insurance policies and your home's equity, there is one more place where people typically borrow their own money and have to pay interest: their retirement 401(k) plans through work.

People will say of these types of loans that the interest they're paying is going right back to them. That may be true, but there's more going on here that is often forgotten. What you might have received in earnings had you left your money inside your plan could have been substantially more. Unlike the life insurance loan, where money seems to be in two places at the same time—remaining inside your policy while also providing a loan outside of your policy—with a 401(k) the money is either inside your plan or outside your plan. This money only does one thing. Your life insurance money does two.

If you take out a retirement account loan you may be enticed to stop or reduce your regular ongoing payroll deduction contributions while you're repaying your loan, thus reducing your expected future values and in doing so, you may be forgoing your company match which could reduce your future values even more.

If your employment is terminated during the duration of the 401(k) loan and you are under the age of 59 ½, you will only have sixty days to repay all the money from the loan or it will be declared as a withdrawal and you could owe all the taxes due from that transaction. You could also be required to pay a tax penalty, as well. In addition, there may be processing fees involved with the loan, and you won't have the flexibility of changing the payment terms until the loan is paid back in full.

But, here is the most important aspect most people neglect to realize when using a loan through an employer's retirement account. The original money in your retirement account coming out in the form of a loan was probably made with pretax contributions.

But, as you pay the loan back into the plan, you're using "after-tax" money. So, the additional cost to this loan is the "spread" or the difference of the cost represented by your tax bracket. In other words, if you're in the thirty percent marginal tax bracket, a contribution which cost you $100 initially to put into your retirement plan, may cost you $143 to put back into your retirement plan a second time by repaying your loan. ($143 − 30% = $100).

Math can be ugly.

# Chapter Fifteen

*"The Colonel"*

The doctors and nurses told us to come quickly. The wires and tubes that had been monitoring and keeping my father-in-law, Bill, alive had been rapidly removed. Now, it would be only minutes.

About an hour earlier, some of us were standing and some were sitting as we discussed as a family the eventual decision that we had hoped we wouldn't have to make. Anne, my mother-in-law, sat quietly listening to the hospital social worker. The rest of us—Betty, her two sisters, Judy and Jane, along with their spouses, and me, in addition to a couple of the older grandchildren—for the moment simply listened and quietly nodded. The hope we had earlier had now faded.

Several weeks earlier, Bill had been in China, and in just a few days he was scheduled to give a business presentation aboard a cruise ship, something he had been looking forward to doing. The doctors couldn't explain what happened, but the death certificate would list a form of pneumonia as the cause of death.

Just weeks before, Bill had entered the hospital, which was very unusual. A businessman and a retired "full bird" colonel from the Army Reserves, the insignia of which is a United States' bald eagle, Bill was just beginning to think about slowing down at the age of seventy-one. In a group, we all called him "Grandpa Bill." One-on-one, for me, it was simply Bill.

-----

I had expected that he and I would have been buddies well into his nineties hitting the roads together bike riding, a passion of his and something I did reluctantly. We would have also continued visiting Civil War sites, which would have provided him the opportunity to share his love of historical battlefield facts. He had always been conscience of his health. He loved to learn, and he loved to teach. When he was a young livestock feed salesman, he claimed that he kept awake at the wheel of his car during long drives by systematically configuring in his mind how he could reengineer his car to be an airplane.

If he learned a new fact or a new quotation, he would share it with everyone within the next several days. Once after having his teeth cleaned, he returned home reminding everyone how his dentist told him to "only floss the teeth you want to keep."

When Betty and I owned our first home, a tiny little house with an unfinished basement, Bill offered to help me build it out before our baby daughter arrived. "Helping me" is a huge understatement! I didn't have a clue. I'm sure Bill came up with the idea himself, realizing as a young couple, we had nowhere to grow with our soon-to-be-expanding family. He offered to make it happen with me taking on the role as a gopher; you know, "go-for-this, go-for-that."

Each week, he would drive from his and Anne's home three hours away and spend the entire weekend helping to build out the basement. Then late each Sunday afternoon, he would write up a list of materials we would need the next weekend for me to pick up at the local lumberyard. Then he would show me some simple carpentry tasks he felt I could do before his next visit without screwing them up too badly.

During the project, he would sometimes pause and look at a pivotal decision that would need to be made before moving on. Taking a breath, he would ask me, "What do you think we should do about" such and such? "Are you kidding me?" I would think to myself. Bill was a vocational/agriculture teacher for four years, after being the first in his family to graduate from college. I, on the other hand had no carpentry skills, at all. But, this was his way of teaching. He wanted to get you to think it through yourself. Eventually, he would say, "What do you think of this idea?" and then continue with the plan he had in his head already from earlier in the day. The basement project probably could have been completed at least one weekend earlier, if Bill hadn't stopped so often to try and teach me something along the way. But the fact of the matter is, I did learn as we spent our time together that late winter and early spring.

Bill also could see things in people that they sometimes couldn't see in themselves. In a prior life, as I sometimes refer to it, I worked in the broadcasting industry beginning at a small market radio station in southern Minnesota as a staff announcer. You could find me broadcasting at the county fair, but mainly it meant sitting in a small room alone reading the news, sports, commercials, and playing music. It was a fun job with very low pay. It wasn't exactly a career that would easily provide for a future family. Bill would say to me, knowing my personality and abilities, "You should get into sales." This is how Bill, himself, had moved up into the corporate world. I remember without even a moment of pause shooting back at him "never," thinking to myself that salespeople were somehow all crooks. But, Bill saw something in me that I couldn't see for myself.

A few years later, the realization came to me that I had an ability to work with people. I felt comfortable listening and finding solutions to people's problems. At one point after making my big career change from broadcasting, Bill told me to never think about sales commissions. "If you do the right thing," he'd say, "you'll always be okay. You won't have to worry about the money." Even though much of my work today is fee-based, his words still ring true with me, "If you do the right thing, you'll always be okay."

-----

When it came time for Bill to retire from the military, an extra job he dearly loved, he would be able to focus all of his time toward the computer-based training company that he and his business partner, Jeanne, had built over the previous couple of decades. Before deciding on how he would take his military pension, he asked me, "Couldn't I get a larger monthly pension amount from the military if I bought a life insurance policy to cover Anne's part of my pension in the event of my death?" "Sure," I replied. "That's called 'pension maximization'." This became one of the first life insurance policies that I wrote on a family member, and it was Bill's idea.

Working with family members can sometimes be a little dicey. Sometimes, the stark truth can be a little too blunt when shared with a close family member, where a regular client can usually accept the same recommendation with much more ease. In the Bible, it says a prophet isn't accepted in his own hometown. That's why with close friends and relatives, I have often waited for them to ask me for advice as opposed to offering it. It can feel like a very fine line to walk, because at the very same time, I also want what's best for those who are closest to me.

Here's how pension maximization works. When soon-to-be retirees have the opportunity to receive a monthly pension, a spousal benefit is usually chosen in the event the primary pensioner dies. To provide a spousal benefit, the primary pensioner has to take a reduction in their own monthly pension amount to provide a secondary pension to their spouse. Since a pension typically lasts for a person's entire lifetime, when two lives are added to the equation it extends the probable time period that the pension will be paid, since now it's based on two lives, not just one. The odds dictate that "one of the two" should live longer than just the "one."

Furthermore, if the pensioner's spouse actually dies first, under most pension arrangements, the primary pensioner continues to receive the lesser amount with no recalculation back to the higher amount they could have received in the first place, without the contingency plan built into the pension arrangement for their spouse. This is the gamble taken when a married couple chooses how they will take a pension. Bill had already run the numbers and thought he would be ahead of the game to take his full pension, while also purchasing a sizable whole life insurance policy in the event that his life expectancy wasn't what he expected it to be.

At the time when we were discussing his pension, Bill also asked Anne to purchase a basic whole life insurance policy through me, as well. Interestingly enough, Anne's father, who she always referred to as "Daddy," had himself been a life insurance agent and had owned his own insurance agency in the state of New Jersey where she and her two sisters had grown up. Her father, James Russell Freeman, had been the last agent to write a policy for her, years before she had married Bill. It was a modest little whole life policy that had paid dividends, year after year. It had performed perfectly, but it was just small. So, the new policy would be in addition to, not in replacement of, the policy that "Daddy" had written on Anne.

-----

In the private hospital waiting room, we continued nodding and listening intently to the hospital social worker. During the last couple weeks, we had seen Bill arrive at the hospital for what we thought would just be a short stay. My wife,

Betty, went up to the hospital to be with her dad and mom to lend encouragement. On the next weekend, I, along with our kids, ages fourteen and seventeen at the time, went up to visit. Betty had asked me to stop by an art supply store along the way to purchase a small erasable white board and marker. Bill had been on a respirator to help his breathing. Though he was now off of the machine, he had difficulty speaking because of the discomfort to his throat while the tube had been in place. At that point, we all had the same thought: When is Bill getting out of this place?

Using the white board, at one point Bill asked Betty why everyone was there, as if he were concerned we knew something he didn't know about his health prognosis. She simply replied, "Of course, we're all here. You're in the hospital, and it's Easter. We want to be with you."

After that day, Bill's health began to change for the worse. Betty stayed nearby with friends and family. I would drive the two and a half hours every couple of days back to the hospital after sending the kids off to school, returning later the same night, trying to make sure they had food to eat, they were completing their school work, and that everything else was under control.

Bill's health deteriorated so much that the doctors placed him back onto a respirator. To do this, they needed to sedate him, which meant that the line of communication between him and the family was now severed. During this time there was someone in the room with him practically every hour of every day. We would wait for the latest x-ray and latest bit of news, any news. We soon came to realize that when doctors didn't have anything new to share or if the news was bad, they would sometimes wait until they knew the family had taken a break for a meal to do their rounds. As Bill got worse, we seemed to see the doctors less and less.

I don't know who said it. I believe it was Anne, verbalizing that Bill wouldn't want to continue this way. We were now at the point where an ultimate decision would have to be made by the family. Since it was late in the afternoon, the social worker said, "We can get the doctors together tomorrow to meet with you." I know I was the one who spoke up next. "There isn't a doctor who can meet with us now?" I asked. "Why should Bill have to stay this way overnight until sometime tomorrow?"

Within a half hour we were talking with the doctor on duty from the ICU, where Bill now laid, kept alive by machines. The doctor talked. We listened. We talked. She listened. The decision was made. We were told to wait near his room.

The doctor and nurses would disconnect all the wires and tubes. They would shutdown the machines that had been forcing air in and out of Bill's lungs. The whir of machines would be quieted. The beeping noises would be silenced, and the display panels would be shut off except for one outside the room on the console at the nurses' station.

We entered the room, now quiet as a chapel. The curtains were closed to the rest of the world. As we circled Bill's hospital bed, we joined hands; we prayed, we cried, and we sang a hymn. Bill's chest rose and fell, rose and fell, and then momentarily quivered as the last remaining breath left his body. We all touched him before leaving the room, touching an arm, a shoulder, or his face for a brief moment of a personal goodbye.

Life is so fragile. Years earlier I witnessed the miracle of watching my own children being born, and I could remember the joy expressed in Bill's and Anne's faces each time they held a brand new grandchild. Now, I had just witnessed another miracle: the miracle of life's ending, when we return to our creator.

-----

After the death of a family member there are all of these puzzle pieces that must quickly come together. I don't fully understand how it happens; it just does. The family must get a boost of adrenaline to make it through. The next several days were a blur. I'm sure some family members could explain all the things that were done and by whom in great detail. I can't begin to comprehend or digest the pieces that were brought together in the short preparation time for Bill's wake and funeral. At the end, I think my friend Bill would have been pleased.

-----

About a week after the funeral the business part of Bill's death began. Bill had been receiving his full military pension for more than a decade. He had expected that his life would have lasted much longer. With his death, the pension ended. But he had purchased a whole life insurance policy before taking his pension to offset Anne's loss if he were to die first. After receiving the death certificate, I assisted Anne in completing the proper forms and submitted the claim to the insurance company. Within a few short weeks, she received the proceeds from that policy.

In addition, Bill and his business partner had acquired life insurance as part of a buy/sell arrangement for their business. Partners in business will often purchase life insurance on one another in the event of an unexpected death. Since the loss of either business partner could have led to financial difficulty regarding the operation of the business, it was put into place to protect each partner's share of the business. Also, with the loss of Bill, the company automatically lost part of its value, which in many cases could affect customer acquisition and maintaining current clients, since Bill worked at attracting and keeping many of the clients the firm worked with.

Likewise, companies can also experience credit difficulties with banks if they have a line of credit. These business arrangements also provide the structure for a buyout arrangement for the deceased's next of kin; in this case, Anne. The cost of the buyout was automatically funded through the purchase of life insurance the business partners had purchased on one another. Bill's partner was able to buy out his share of the business from Anne by using the buy/sell insurance proceeds in an amount they had predetermined and made formal with a legal document prepared years earlier with an attorney.

Small companies or partnerships facing the same circumstances without a life insurance funded buy/sell arrangement may find the remaining partner(s) now forced to work with a surviving spouse who has no personal interest in the business. The company or surviving partners could be forced to take out substantial bank loans to buy out the deceased partner's next of kin, or they may find the financial burden to the company so great that they have to close down the business altogether. Since the correct steps had been planned out ahead of time, within a month of Bill's death the business continuation and ownership changes had been resolved.

Life insurance is the perfect product that provides the money you need, at exactly the time that you need it. For Anne, it provided the replacement for the pension she lost at Bill's death. For Jeanne, Bill's business partner, it provided the money to buy out his portion of the business and keep the company up and running, also giving Anne the financial equivalent of Bill's share of the company he had founded.

-----

A couple of months before Bill's death, Betty and I had purchased a small tract of land along the Flambeau River in northern Wisconsin. We hoped that in the future we would build a small cabin getaway. We emailed photos of the land we had bought to Bill. The pictures were mostly of trees, some shoreline, and the river. We finally built our cabin about eight years after Bill's death. In the interim, we roughed it like pioneers with a small ten-by-fourteen foot Amish built bunkhouse and a matching outhouse. We admit to ourselves that if Bill were alive, we probably would have built the cabin much sooner, because he would have relished the thought of driving up each weekend, trying to teach me how to build a cabin. Bill never saw our little piece of land in person. But, when we emptied out the trunk of his car after this death, we found a manila file with copies of the photos we had emailed to him, which he had printed off on a color printer.

There are two massive bald eagle nests, where the majestic adults raise their young, about a half-mile upstream from our river property. When we sit by our fire pit watching the cool water slowly easing downstream, especially in the early morning hours when the green colors of the trees and the blue sky above reflects brilliantly against the river, a bald eagle will sometimes quietly glide by with its huge wings extended seven feet from tip to tip. Betty or I always pause, then quietly say to one another, "There goes the Colonel."

# Chapter Sixteen

*"What's left?"*

It doesn't matter who we are, we all will be leaving something of financial value on the table at the moment of our death. If you're reading this book, you may have already acquired some assets during your lifetime. Perhaps they're substantial. Perhaps they're still modest.

When we die, there is almost always "something left on the table" to pass onto loved ones. I experienced this firsthand by receiving a small share of a great aunt's estate when she passed away well into her nineties. I grew up knowing her as "Aunt Ex"—a shortened version of her given name, Exerine. She and her husband, Germaine, never had any children of their own. As a schoolteacher, Aunt Ex had been a saver her entire life. She began her career in the same one-room schoolhouse my father attended when he started grade school. I remember visiting Ex on a Thanksgiving Day, years ago, as she was spending her last days in a nursing home. The staff asked if I wanted to feed her the simple Thanksgiving Day meal they had prepared that day at the nursing facility.

It provides a different perspective when you realize that the person you're feeding was someone who probably held you in her arms, holding a bottle for you when you were an infant. Now, in a moment, the roles were reversed. I didn't know that Ex had any money, so it came as a surprise when my mother, who acted as her executor, informed me and my siblings, as great-nephews and nieces, that we were named in her will.

When you have something of value wouldn't you like to pass it along to your loved ones? If possible, wouldn't you wish to pass the most you could, while also enjoying the fruits of your labor while you are still alive?

If you are young and have yet to build your future wealth, you need to begin deciding now what assets you wish to hold and how those assets may give you the security for now, for your future, and for your family when you are no longer here.

-----

Humorously, I will sometimes share my perfect financial plan with clients:

"The day I die, I want to be overdrawn at the bank (which means I spent and enjoyed all of my money while I was still alive), and then I want the very last check that I write against my account to be written to the IRS, and I want that check to bounce!"

After the laugh that I usually receive from clients, I then pause and become very serious and continue on. "Then I want my life insurance to recreate all the money I had spent during my entire lifetime, so my family can do it all over again."

Seriously, think about it. Wouldn't that be the very best plan that you could ever imagine? Here's the thing though—it would be virtually impossible to do, though not for the reason you might expect. The reason is that we're all afraid of running out of money before we run out of life. So, in almost all likelihood, you and I are going to be leaving something "on the table" after our death. The question that needs to be posed is what is the best asset to leave behind?

After the funeral for my father-in-law, Bill, the work really began on the process of settling his estate, which meant organizing and retitling assets. The will Bill and Anne had drawn up years earlier was very simple in nature. I refer to straightforward wills such as they had, as "I love you" wills; meaning if I die, you get all my stuff, and if you die, I get all your stuff. It's all pretty black and white, but the first question after a death is typically "What's the stuff and where is it?"

Life insurance had replaced the lost income of Bill's pension, and life insurance had taken care of Bill's ownership interest in the company he started years earlier with Jeanne, his business partner. Life insurance is easy. It's the other stuff that's hard.

As expected, my mother-in-law, Anne, was named as the executor of Bill's estate. Having grown up during a time when men typically took care of a family's finances, I didn't know how much Anne knew about the intricacies of the retirement accounts or other investments Bill may have acquired over the years. Since I was the financial advisor in the family, I was "up to bat," as it were. The rest of the family seemed relieved when I said I would help Anne through this process.

Over the next couple of months I would leave home early on Friday mornings, drive three hours to Anne's home, spending the day organizing documents and files and return home that same evening. One of the first Fridays, Anne and I met with their attorney to receive a list of what was needed to properly complete tax returns and property retitling. The attorney also discussed updating Anne's will to document her estate wishes moving forward. Anne began going through boxes at home looking for documents, making sure that we didn't overlook something important.

My job began at Bill's office, which had remained untouched except for office staff retrieving client folders from his desk. I visited with his business partner, Jeanne, the first Friday I arrived at their offices. I inquired how she was holding up, after having lost her business partner, and how the rest of the staff was doing. We had our serious moments and shared a few humorous stories about Bill, as well. She knew that I had arrived to clean out Bill's corner office, so she provided me with a box of large black plastic garbage bags. As she handed it to me, she remarked, "Good luck."

Even though I had been advising clients for years, I felt that this was really my first personal experience on the front lines, as it were. It's a lot easier to explain how to organize an estate. It's a much different process of actually doing it. I opened Bill's walnut office door, walked around to his side of the desk and sat in his chair looking at his nearly untouched desk with the backdrop of his favorite color—baby blue—that he had painted on his office walls himself. The curtain covering Bill's windows looking out onto the island of cubicles and the rest of the office was closed so I wouldn't be disturbed nor would the employees be bothered watching me clean out the office of their company's founder. I sat there and sighed.

I had only been in Bill's office a very few times, and I had never been on this side of his desk before. As I looked across the top of his desk, I rubbed my face with both hands and asked myself, where do I begin? There were two empty cardboard boxes in the corner of the room, so I decided one would be for his personal items, one would be for financial documents, and anything else would be thrown away in the garbage bags Jeanne had given me. If you believe that this should be a relatively simple straightforward task, then you need to take a look around your own home. It's not.

Some decisions were easy–packet of gum, garbage. A statement with a bunch of numbers couldn't be categorized so quickly. What was the date of the statement? Did it indicate something that still existed? Who do I call to find out? Where's the telephone number? Will they give me any information over the telephone? If they don't, how do I receive the authorization for them to release the information? I would look at each piece of paper and ask myself, "Is this something or is this nothing?"

By four o'clock that first day, which was the amount of time I had budgeted, the personal effects box was partially full, the document box was partially full, and I had filled two large garbage bags which I took out to the dumpster in back of the Main Street office building. I would return for three more Fridays before only the two boxes remained and everything else had been cleared from Bill's office. You might be thinking that Bill was a packrat. He wasn't, though he did have items dating from throughout his life since his college days. Sometimes, I would find envelopes of family photos, so I found myself stopping, reliving family memories; other times, I simply needed to pause and catch my breath remembering that Bill was gone. Occasionally, thankful that the door was closed, I complained out loud to Bill about all the work I was doing, and if he would have just lived, everything could just be the way that it was, but it wasn't.

-----

Eventually, we were able to secure all the documents we needed, tallying up the assets and completing the settlement of the estate. One of the reasons I love using life insurance as an estate planning tool is because the money is there right when you need it and at a predetermined amount. So, you know what the amount is going to be and you don't have to wait a long period of time to get it. In my opinion, it really is the perfect asset.

A couple of the assets Anne was now responsible for were two rental properties. These properties had been wonderful investments for Bill. He bought them cheap, put a lot of his own sweat-equity into them, and he had also pulled money out of them over the years for business purposes or other uses. But when he died they both had loans against them, which is not unusual at all for real estate investors, since profit is determined by the spread between what you owe each month and what you receive in rents each month. Well managed, business loans can have some very positive benefits for the investor.

Here's the problem, though. Anne wasn't a real estate investor, and she just wanted out of them. Unfortunately, because of a downturn in the real estate market at the time and unusually high gasoline prices making their location less favorable for commuters, the properties just sat. It took more than a year to finally sell each property, after the modest selling price on each had been lowered several times.

-----

Bill and Anne's situation reflects that of many couples regarding their estates. What are the best assets to leave on the table, at your death?

Real estate?

It depends. Will there be a loan against the real estate or will it be debt-free? Is it being rented or is it empty? Does the person inheriting it understand real estate investing? If the property takes a long time to sell, is there enough money available to pay for the real estate taxes, insurance, water/sewer and electric bills until it is sold? What happens if the real estate market is at a downturn and it needs to be sold at a loss? What if you wish to wait to sell it? Is there enough money to pay all the bills until the market turns around and what will those costs be and for how long?

What about your own home?

Are your kids on the same page? Do they get along? Will they be able to work together? Does your house need updating before it's sold? Is there money to do the updates? Is there money to pay for its upkeep until it's sold? Can your kids agree on a realtor? Will your kids be able to agree on a price? How about if one of your kids really needs the money now and the other doesn't. Does that change how quickly the property will be sold and at what price?

How about inheriting a 401(k), traditional IRA, or other qualified plan?

A spouse can receive these assets "in transfer" without paying income taxes with that transfer, but eventually distributions from these plans are taxed as taxable income. If your children inherit one of these plans there are some fancy ways to initially delay taxation for a time, though the government keeps entertaining ways to limit these exceptions. But, this also limits your heirs' access to this money. You may be leaving them money they can't use in the way you intended.

These plans may play out very poorly as an estate-planning tool. Let's say you die at a nice old age. If that's the case, your kids are now probably at the highest income earning years of their lifetime. Let's say you have three kids and your $300,000 retirement plan "inheritance" throws them into as much as a 40 percent marginal bracket, between federal and state income taxes. You thought your three kids would each receive $100,000. But, because of taxes the government might get $120,000 and each of your three kids receive only $60,000. The government has possibly become your single largest beneficiary. Plus, there's still the worry if these assets are in the stock market. What will be the value of those investments on the day they're liquidated? If you had owned a boring $300,000 whole life insurance policy, your kids would have potentially received $100,000 each, income tax free.

What about your brokerage or Roth IRA accounts?

Have the brokerage accounts been titled properly or will they have to go through probate? Are the Roth IRA beneficiary designations correctly documented? How long will the process take to liquidate the brokerage account? What happens if the stock market is at a low at the time of your death? What happens if the stock market drops while your heirs are waiting to liquidate or transfer these accounts? Are the accounts protected against loss?

If a whole life policy is properly created, the process is simple. At the time of death, the coroner completes a death certificate. Once a certified copy is obtained and provided with a death claim form to the insurance company, they'll complete the paperwork in just a couple of weeks and will pay out the death benefit income tax-free in addition to any paid-up additional insurance the policy may have accumulated through dividends, in addition to any unused premiums (refunded), in addition to any interest earned from the date of death through the date the check was made out to the named beneficiaries: a known amount, risk-free and probate-free, at exactly the time it is needed.

-----

When Bill's estate had finally been settled, the tax forms completed, and the rental properties sold, we as a family could finally begin to move forward. The first time we came together for a holiday celebration, Anne and Bill's dining room table was extended into the living room as it always was for family get-togethers, so everyone would have a seat at the same table. As the table laid set for the meal and each of us still bustling around with the last minute details of garnishes and side dishes, I motioned to Anne and quietly said, "You know, you need to sit at the head of the table." It had always been Bill's spot. She answered "I thought one of you guys (meaning a son-in-law) would sit there." "No, Anne," I replied. "You need to sit at the head of the table. It's your place now."

Anne took her time to settle into her new role without Bill. I would drive over each March thereafter and spend the morning with her organizing tax documents so we could meet with her CPA to complete her tax return for the past year. Each year the documenting would become less complicated. She would have neat little piles of tax forms waiting for me on the dining room table along with a sharpened pencil, paper, and a small adding machine. After I had sorted everything out during the morning, we would go to the local Chinese or pizza buffet before driving downtown to complete her taxes with her accountant.

Anne had always wanted a white house. She got it one year when the family spent a weekend covering over the olive green paint that had been there since she, Bill, and the girls moved to this small Midwestern town from the outskirts of Little Rock, Ark., decades earlier.

Anne and Betty took a trip together to France. Anne had always wanted to see Paris in the springtime. Together, they enjoyed a luxury tour with great sights and wonderful food. During the trip, Anne even cheated on the diet her doctor had prescribed due to a heart ailment that was kept in check by a pacemaker and medication.

After awhile, the house was becoming too large to manage, and Anne began to think she would be ready now, with the passage of time, to move to a condominium where everything would be on one floor, and the condo fees would take away the responsibility of having to hire out the mowing and the snow plowing for the house. Over time, the three daughters helped to downsize Anne's belongings preparing for the move to the condo.

Nearly every night, Anne would visit with one of her sisters who lived on the East Coast, by telephone. After not hearing from Anne for a couple of days, her sister Peg became concerned and called Judy, one of the daughters. At the house, newspapers were found piled up near the entry. It appeared that Anne had prepared herself for bed one night, slipped under the covers, and simply gone to sleep. There appeared to be no trauma; during the night, she just quietly slipped away. Anne was 78 years old.

The small whole life policy which "Daddy," her father, had purchased for Anne when she wasn't yet an adult and the whole life policy I had written for her twenty-two years earlier did exactly what they had been planned for, paying a dividend each year and increasing their values for this moment.

Investments Don't Hug

# Chapter Seventeen

*What does an illustration really show?*

Looking back over my three-decade career, I realize how very little I knew in the beginning. I haven't just come to that conclusion. I grasped how naive I was early on. After acquiring all the required licenses, the regulators said I was "legally" ready.

But, I wasn't. There was this constant fear of not doing my absolute best. Trying to help a client navigate through decisions that could impact them for the rest of their lives was daunting. I took little comfort from a manager who said to me, "Whatever you do, they'll be better off than if they had never met you." That didn't really make me feel any more confident at the time, but when I visit with those first clients today, it sometimes amazes me how those few little baby steps I took years ago have now been transformed into a confident stride.

This can be somewhat daunting in any profession. As a doctor goes through a residency program, they will sometimes refer to the mantra of "Watch one, do one, teach one," which describes how each resident watches a procedure being performed on a live patient for the first time. Then they perform that procedure on the next available patient themselves, followed by teaching that same procedure to the next resident. The financial services industry and many other businesses work exactly the same way. Though I was trying my best, at least I didn't have to worry that a misstep could kill someone.

I realized early on that the company I was working for brought in as many new hires as possible only to see who would stick. Using the law of large numbers, it was thought if enough young guys and gals were thrown against the wall, at some point enough of them would remain. In the beginning, the company I worked for financed a basic income level of compensation. But, within a couple of years keeping your job and your income was based on the work you did and your success in building a base of clients. At the end of my second year, I kept my job by the skin of my teeth, or actually by $127. After an entire two years, my future may have been determined by my own profitability of $127.

Realizing early that the manager was working on a numbers game of new hires and not on how well we did our jobs, I took the initiative to seek out additional education outside the sphere of what the company and, obviously, the local office would provide. In fact, within a relatively short period of time spent in industry, association, and designation programs, I comfortably felt that I had outgrown my current environment and knew more than my manager, since he was really just a company recruiter. What I had learned in that office setting I would frequently refer to as "one year of experience, eight years in a row."

So, with a giant gulp and an $8,000 personal bank loan, I stepped out on my own to a one-room basement office. Even though those beginnings were modest, the reach for knowledge continued and still remains an important part of my professional growth. There are inexpensive ways to earn required continuing education. But, you get what you pay for. Instead, just as in the beginning of my career, I still worry about doing the absolutely best I can for each client and that can't be accomplished for clients 'on the cheap.'

-----

With knowledge comes the assertiveness to challenge conventional wisdom. The usual wisdom when I was young persuaded me to believe that the stock market would always experience regular double-digit increases. That's what I grew up with. This would become the first lesson. Only three weeks into my first month in the financial services industry, the stock market, as measured by the Dow Jones Industrial average fell by more than twenty percent in just one day. They called it "Black Monday." The belief in gradual, predictable market movements could now be scratched off the list.

During the tech bubble of the '90s, many stockbrokers shared with me that their clients threatened to pull all their accounts from them if their money wasn't invested fully into the aggressive growth stocks that were reaching new highs daily at the time. For fear of losing their clients, the brokers did exactly as they were told to do by their clients, and then they watched their clients assets disappear anyway.

After the Y2K computer scare, the tragedy of Sept. 11, 2001, occurred, and then the world was overcome by the effects of the Great Recession. The first ten years of the new century became known as the lost decade, since many people ended the decade with no more money in their investment accounts than there had been ten years earlier.

-----

This may seem like a very long preamble to explain the tool used by the life insurance industry to demonstrate how their products work. But it's important to begin with a historical perspective.

The tool is called an illustration. Before laptops, life insurance was primarily explained conceptually. When I began my career, to generate an illustration meant "running the numbers" through a desktop computer. These illustrations most often though are misunderstood by the public and are often also misunderstood by the agents who use them. For many years prior to regulatory changes requiring an insured to formally sign illustrations as part of the compliance procedures to purchase life insurance, I seldom showed one to a client because of the immediate misunderstanding of how illustrations are to be used. Instead, I preferred to review the actual life insurance contract, since that was actually what was being purchased, not the illustration.

Watching agents discussing the comparison of one policy over another, I would often shake my head back and forth.

Here's the thing about "the numbers." The life insurance company knows all the moving parts. They know your chance of dying. They know their administrative costs, and they know their expected investment returns. There is no "special deal" from one whole life policy over another. The pricing and the benefits are tweaked to accomplish what the insured is trying to accomplish.

Actuarially, one policy with the same company is essentially equal with other policies of the same company. So, if one is cheaper (let's say, "less expensive"), then some benefit has been taken away from it; and for the general public, just what is missing is sometimes hard to find. You may immediately see the difference between a Cadillac and a Chevy, but with a life insurance policy the differences are more difficult to delineate for the novice.

Here is how an illustration should be used. A whole life illustration "illustrates" how a policy would perform today and moving forward until the insured person reaches the age of 121, assuming—this is the key—nothing else ever changes. Nothing! For the rest of time, all the elements that are credited to the policy never change. Remember, there are three basic elements of a whole life insurance policy. The illustrations are based on the assumption that:

- Portfolio returns which are keyed into fixed rates of return **never change**.
- Mortality experience, meaning the chances of dying by the general public, **never change**.
- Administrative expenses of the life insurance company's policies **never change**.

I can think of very few things in my life that didn't change within the past month, let alone over years. But, now a client might be making a decision on the success of a policy based on nothing changing for the next ten, twenty, thirty, or forty years!

Here's how silly this is. Our first home mortgage loan rate, when Betty and I were in our 20s, was at a rate of 10.7 percent. Our last home mortgage rate was 2.7 percent. If I'm trying to do a long-term projection for the future, which one should I use? During my lifetime, both have been correct.

If I was making a projection that couldn't change at some time in the future, which Dow Jones Industrial Average rates of return would I use? Do I use the annual rate of return from 2008, which was -33.84 percent or do I use the annual rate of return from 2013, which was +26.50 percent? That is a difference of 60.34 percentage points. Which one is the correct one? They both are!

Would I use either and project it out for the next ten, twenty, thirty, or forty years? Of course not. In reply, you might suggest for me to use an average set of returns over a longer period of time. Then we would have to argue over which average should we use; what length of time we should stipulate? But, here's the key—whole life insurance illustrations don't use "averages." They are only allowed, by regulation, to show "at this very moment in time," illustrated ahead without any changes, whatsoever, as to rates of return, mortality experience, and administrative costs, all of which are virtually guaranteed to change.

Here is why whole life insurance illustrations changed in the first decade of the twenty-first century:

- Interest rates reached historical lows to near zero during the Great Recession.
- Mortality experience improved so dramatically, as we've already learned, that insurance companies were required to change their endowment ages on whole life policies from age 100 to age 121.
- Administrative costs dropped substantially due to new computing capabilities and access via the internet.

I am amazed, with all of the ongoing changes in today's world, that actuaries are able to price out policies at all. But, some United States companies have been successfully doing so for more than 150 years.

When you review a life insurance illustration, note the wording of the text on the document. Regarding dividends it may state something like: "This illustration assumes that the current dividend schedule will continue unchanged for all the years shown. This is not likely to occur and actual results may be more or less favorable."

*ILLUSTRATIONS ARE NOT PROJECTIONS.*

I needed to capitalize the previous sentence to make this point. If you would use a whole life insurance illustration as a projection, then you would also have to compare it to every other product "frozen in time." Let's pretend it's 2008. We would have to compare the whole life insurance policy to an annualized -33.84 percent return in the Dow

Jones Industrial Average for the rest of time. "Well, that's not fair," you would exclaim. Exactly! That's my point.

Or we could compare the whole life insurance policy to an annualized +26.50 percent rate of return from 2013 for the rest of time. You would say, "That's not going to happen." And again, I would say, "Exactly!" That's why any future projection is really a guessing game; and that's why illustrations are not projections.

A better reason to use an illustration would be to show how dividends *may* be paid in the future, how those dividends *might* be used to purchase additional paid-up insurance, and how that additional insurance *may* accumulate over time to affect your policy beyond the guaranteed values set forth inside the life insurance policy.

Whole life insurance is a steady predictable asset with built-in guarantees. It's a place to put your "safe money" and to take advantage of the other features to make your overall financial planning better. A superior question to ask your financial representative or life insurance agent, when discussing life insurance is to ask, "Without the use of an illustration, can you explain to me how this will make life for me and my family better today and into the future?"

# Chapter Eighteen

*"Keeping your dignity."*

Bill and Penny seemed just like a couple of kids when we first met. They were twenty-eight years old and married only a couple of years. We visited shortly after their son, Jesse, was born. Their home was situated on a long narrow lot with a stand of old woodland trees to the rear of their property. It was a nice spot, nearly in the center of town. Bill was a hunter with a tan complexion, dark hair, and a muscular build. He had an old pole building out back, which stored his hunting gear and other outdoor "man-toys." His favorite colors would have been a mixture of camo and blaze orange. When he wasn't working, Bill longed to be outdoors.

Penny remembers that I told her and Bill to purchase life insurance during our very first visit together. "Thank God, you did," she said, "because we probably never would have, otherwise."

During that first evening we were able to increase Bill's life insurance coverage ten-fold. But, as important as the life insurance was, there were two additional boxes we checked off on their policy applications, to enhance the coverage for each of them. First was a waiver of premium benefit rider, and the second, an accelerated death benefit rider.

The waiver of premium benefit rider would allow their policies to be paid in the event of a disability. The insurance company would become responsible for paying the premiums as they came due.

The accelerated death benefit rider on the other hand, began appearing as an option for most life insurance policies during the late 1980s because of the concern of those who had contracted HIV/AIDS. It became a way to alleviate some of the financial pressures of those who were suffering from the disease, which at that time offered little hope for treatment and virtually guaranteed a death sentence.

The provision for these accelerated "living benefits" could be included in a policy at the time it was issued and under some circumstances, could be added later on. Ordinarily, a life insurance policy pays benefits to a beneficiary after the insured dies. This option allowed for a portion of those benefits to be accelerated in the event of a terminal illness, usually lasting twelve months or less.

Bill had a job in sales. Penny worked as a daycare provider. They added a daughter, Cassie, to their family two years later.

I'm sure those two boxes checked on Bill's life insurance application were soon forgotten as the couple raised their young family. The life insurance was simply for that rare, unexpected death that none of us wish to think about.

-----

Sometimes, life insurance can be much more than an eventual death benefit.

Less than a decade after our first visit, Bill became permanently disabled due to the effects from an inoperable brain tumor. He was thirty-six. Radiation and chemotherapy shrank the cancer by about twenty percent, but surgeons couldn't remove the tumor due to its location. He would have to learn to live with the fact that this cancer had intertwined itself into his life and that of his family just as it had intertwined itself in his brain.

By now, Penny had graduated with a university degree and was working as a special education teacher. Bill had taken a job as a manager for a semi-truck tire company, but that was now in jeopardy due to the seizures he experienced and the short-term memory loss that was a side effect of the cancer.

Yet, Bill continued on; and so did his life insurance policy. But, now it continued without any additional premiums being paid out of pocket by Bill. After submitting a disability claim form, the insurance company activated the waiver of premium benefit. Bill never paid another life insurance premium. A simple box checked off on his life insurance application eliminated the need to pay any more premiums out of his own pocket.

Cancer is frustrating. It obviously has its own timetable, but Bill's determination kept it at bay. We would visit occasionally even though his policy was, for all purposes, on an "auto-pilot" mode. Our next serious visit wouldn't happen until eight years after his diagnosis.

-----

During those interim years, Bill's health would swing wildly. Short-term memory loss and abrupt mood swings became frustrating for his family. Then there was the aftermath of one particular day that Bill spent hunting on the backwaters of the Mississippi River.

That's when Bill contracted West Nile virus, which is transmitted by mosquitoes. Most people infected with West Nile may not experience any signs or symptoms, at all; or they might experience only a fever and a mild headache. Some though, may develop a life-threatening illness, which includes an inflammation of the brain. Bill's brain had already been under attack and fighting its own war for years due to the cancer. Now, it was under attack by a new enemy.

Bill's symptoms came on much like stomach flu with some shaking and a fever. At one point in the middle of the night, he fell down the hallway at home. When Penny took his temperature, it read 105.5.

She called 911 and firemen arrived to carry him from the house by ambulance to an emergency room. By now, Bill was delirious and his temperature was spiking at 108.5. They induced a coma and iced his naked body. The room was bone-chilling cold as they continued applying cooling blankets, fighting to get his fever down.

As I visited with Penny later, I said, "He should have died," under those circumstances. She replied, "A part of him wished he would have."

-----

Initially, the West Nile virus left Bill paralyzed. During this time, Penny continued to work fulltime, attending school to further her education, and doing a couple of home shows each week for a multilevel marketing company to add to Bill's monthly Social Security disability benefits. Later, Penny would also tutor students three days a week.

Bill was hospitalized for three and a half months. When he returned home, friends and family would come and stay with him. Penny would make sure he was toileted and showered before leaving for work. He was in a wheelchair then. It would be another three to four months before he was able to walk once more. At the same time, the brain cancer had now been with Bill for eight years.

"He had a rough time," Penny said. "At the time, the doctors gave him three to five years."

Penny continued on with her education, earning a master's degree, and accepting a position as a second grade teacher. "Being a second grade teacher is filled with rainbows, sunshine, and hugs every day," she said. "It's wonderful!"

But, there was another part of her life that wasn't wonderful. There was a dark time during Bill's illness when he and Penny separated. Penny remembers that the only reason for their separation was because Bill couldn't manage being a father. "It wasn't his fault," she says. "Depression and brain cancer changes who you are mentally, and then the radiation can do that too. Then add the West Nile virus on top of everything. All of that, and it became more and more difficult."

It all just drained Bill mentally. Eventually, Bill became like a twelve–year-old boy, only watching television and playing video games all day long, while growing increasingly angry. Penny shared that she and Bill were blessed that their kids, who were by then a senior and sophomore in high school, were so understanding and accepting, because they had every reason not to be.

During their separation, Bill lived with his aging mother, but he received ongoing care from his family. With time, he gained his strength back.

He felt better as his seizures became less frequent. But, he had begun losing the use of one of his legs, which he would drag along behind as he walked. Because of this, he experienced multiple falls. He agreed to go into a nursing home, to try rehabilitation. It was then that their doctor scheduled an MRI. When brain cancer begins to encroach further, a patient's seizures may sometimes end. Unfortunately, that was the case with Bill.

-----

It was decided that Bill would initially return home for hospice care. The kids and Penny had learned to keep their home functioning by themselves. So, Penny made a deal with Bill that he would come home, but that he wouldn't take on the role of parenting. He was okay with that plan. Penny and Bill were now both forty-three. The additional concern for Bill's return home included their daughter Cassie's anxiety of seeing her dad suffer. Jesse, their son, on the other hand, feared the uncontrolled emotional rants he had experienced from his father earlier, as Bill lost the battle for the control over his brain.

Penny recalled when she and Bill first applied for his disability benefits; it brought tears to their doctor's eyes. "It's been a relationship," Penny said. "It's been eight years!" she continued. "Bill and I remembered the pregnancies and births which our doctor had gone through, while she was also caring for us."

"So, when it came time to have the discussion about hospice, our doctor had to be very clear to Bill. When she said the word hospice, I knew what that meant, but I didn't think Bill knew, so I said 'Will you explain to Bill what hospice means?'."

Their doctor explained: "It's special caring for people, when we expect that they will live less than six months."

"He needed that to be said, that clearly and that directly," Penny knew.

"When the doctor finished with her explanation, Bill broke down and cried and then our doctor started crying too. She excused herself. The social worker in the room said, 'She's just having a hard time.' I totally understood; we'd known each other for eight years. It's not easy to tell somebody they are going to die at the age of forty-three."

-----

Over the years, I had several discussions about the accelerated death benefit rider on Bill's policy. Upon approval by the insurance company, it would allow a prepayment of part of Bill's death benefit prior to his death. This time, I began the conversation with a question, "Are you guys thinking of traveling somewhere?"

"I don't know," replied Penny. "Bill would like to go four-wheeling sooner than later. That's Bill!"

"I think he would love to find somewhere that had the facilities so he could go and shoot something. Bill just wants to do something fun. But, each day he's becoming weaker and weaker. I've got to get the ball rolling," she ended.

We filled out the insurance forms together and I gave copies for Penny to take to Bill's doctor, to be completed.

When Penny came into my office to pick up the accelerated death benefit payment, Bill could no longer speak and the right side of his body was now paralyzed.

When I had last spoken with Penny, she said that they were making plans to travel to Florida and use a condo a friend had offered them. But, as those few weeks passed, Bill had lost the use of his arm and he expressed it would be too difficult to travel. Penny told me that she needed him to verbalize that. She didn't want to be the one to curb his wishes.

Instead, he would use his remaining time writing each of their children a letter and having their pastor read them aloud, since he no longer could. Bill had his wedding ring melted down and had a special ring made for his daughter. He chose a headstone, had their house reroofed, and saw other projects completed around the house.

Perhaps the accelerated death benefit didn't offer the one last trip for the family. But what it did supply was supplementary funds that allowed Bill to keep his dignity, providing a sense of control over some of the final aspects of his life.

-----

Some months after Bill's death, Penny and I visited about what she had learned through this experience.

"What have I learned?" Penny repeated back to me. "That life insurance is totally necessary. Just knowing that it was there, eased my mind. Because, if the worst happens, I knew we'd be okay financially. I can't imagine having gone through this and not having life insurance and thinking what if I had all those bills and no way of paying them. I have also learned about family and how to deal with doctors and institutions. I feel like I should have a different job sometimes because I know how to advocate for families because of the amounts of time we have spent in the hospital.

"I've see the way some medical staff will dismiss families and won't acknowledge you when you walk into the room. The hospital had students coming into our room when Bill was there for the West Nile virus. He was on a ventilator and someone would come in and ask him how his hunting season was, because they could see he was a hunter, since we had pictures up all over the room. He couldn't answer. You shouldn't be asked open-ended questions in that situation. Instead, talk to the family and ask what types of communication would work best. Learn from the family; just little things like that.

"Now, I've become this person that everyone calls when they know somebody who has a cancer diagnosis. I get random phone calls. A friend of mine's husband was just diagnosed and I called them and talked to them about how you can get ninety days' worth of prescription drugs for the same price as thirty, especially if it's a prescription you are going to be using often. Done right, you only have the expense of one co-payment, not three. There are all these little nuances no one ever tells you about. It's the little things that make your life easier. It's like you've had a tornado rip through your life and you now speak a language that nobody else understands."

Penny's wisdom is something everyone should consider, not only for their own "what ifs" but to know how to support others going through medical traumas.

"When friends want to bring meals over for the family, don't send crock pots; because, now they have to wash them and figure out how to return them. Instead, give gift cards for food to be delivered to their home; or only provide meals every other day in a throw-away dish, because there's too much food otherwise and a family can't possibly eat it all. Ask the family what they need.

"Consider giving gas cards, because they need to drive back and forth to appointments. This has really given me a very different perspective on everything—to be honest and to cherish. I would say live every day to its fullest, but that's not a reality when you're in the middle of all this stuff; it's just not! You are just trying to survive to the next day.

"I think the biggest lesson that I have learned is the importance of my faith. I am so grateful for my faith. When I'm walking alone I struggle, yet as soon as I reach out and say 'Lord, I need your help,' he's always there. As soon as I am walking alone and I'm comfortable once more, I pull back again and think I can do it on my own. That's my biggest struggle; learning that I can't. God keeps whacking me upside the head, reminding me of that."

-----

Shortly after Bill's funeral, Penny took a trip to Orange County, California. She spent the evenings overlooking the ocean. "It was exactly what I needed," she said. "When I got there, I walked into my hotel room, I put Pandora music on with my little Bluetooth speakers, and then turned on the fireplace and sat down. The first song that came on was the one chosen for Bill's funeral, 'When I Get To Where I'm Going,' sung by Brad Paisley. The next was a song by Alison Krauss: 'When You Say Nothing At All,' which we had danced to at our wedding."

As she sat there alone and wept, perhaps Bill was saying everything was okay.

When Penny returned, she shared the following with me:

"I went to watch the sunset every night, down at the beach and wrote in my journal. I just had 'me time' and I spent the time absorbing what I had just been through in my life. Now, I'm back to work fulltime." Quietly she said, "I made it. Sometimes, people will say that I don't cry; but I do. I cry with my kids."

# Chapter Nineteen

*"The reason for thanksgiving."*

It was one week before Thanksgiving when Scott applied for his life insurance policy. Insurance agents love to complete applications on young, healthy people. Out of the twenty-nine health questions I asked, Scott answered "no" to all of them but one: Was he taking any prescription medications? Yes, tetracycline for some mild acne. Otherwise, Scott was young, strong, and healthy. This is usually the time of life when we all feel invincible, because typically we're all young, strong, and healthy. So, why would Scott need life insurance now?

Having been married for three years, Scott and Jen were in their mid-twenties and wanted to start a family. Jen's dad told her that the best thing a person could do was to prepare for the future, "and they prepared very well for mine," she said of her parents. "I think by taking out the life insurance policy on both of us, we were preparing for something that hopefully, we would never need. Yet, we understood that we had to have it. So, I think when we made that purchase it was because it was something my dad had said that if you had the opportunity, do it." The next thing on their list was a will. She continued, "You do all this paperwork and you prepare for later on, you can't wait until you become sick (to do it)."

Scott was quickly approved for six times more life insurance coverage than what we were replacing, which he had purchased five years earlier before marrying Jen. Usually, I frown on canceling one policy over another and instead prefer to build an insurance portfolio for clients, similar to an investment portfolio. But, they needed more coverage with modest premiums, which would also allow Jen to purchase her own life insurance policy two months later, while keeping within their budget.

Their first daughter, Kaylee, arrived the following year, three days after Thanksgiving. Madisyn, their second daughter arrived four years later, a week after Thanksgiving.

It was difficult for me to imagine that fifteen years after our initial start of this journey together, Jen would find herself at Scott's side holding his hand for the very last time, one day after Thanksgiving.

Perhaps, Thanksgiving would sum up how Scott would want others to remember his life—like the love and fellowship found around the fall holiday table with its blessings of thankfulness and the comfort of familiar smells and tastes and shared times together as family.

-----

Scott and Jen knew one another throughout most of their youth, but they weren't high school sweethearts. Scott lived just outside the city limits to the north of their small rural community. They would see one another when their families went out for Friday night fish frys, a tradition popular across Wisconsin, and they would sometimes spend time together as friends, as kids in small towns do. "Scott would bike into town, and I would be at the city park," Jen remembers. "We would hang out together, but never dated. I attended the public school. Scott attended the local Lutheran school, so we didn't run into one another every day," Jen said. "During high school, Scott's sister Sherrie and my brother Terry dated for three years."

They wouldn't attend school together until high school. As seniors, she was a cheerleader; he played on the basketball team.

"Scott was kind of a dorky, quiet, and reserved kid, feeling more comfortable staying to himself. He loved basketball. So, as a cheerleader, I saw him pretty regularly then. But, I didn't really think much of it. There wasn't a spark back then, and besides, Scott was dating someone else during high school and so was I," she recalls.

"I asked Scott to our senior homecoming dance," Jen said, explaining how it was the girl's responsibility to ask the boys, and it was tradition for cheerleaders and players to attend the dance together. "I actually asked Scott's girlfriend for permission to ask Scott to the dance. We went and had a good time."

Later, after graduation, when neither was dating, Scott was asked by his sister, "Why don't you ask Jen to a movie?"

"So, we went," Jen remembered, becoming very thoughtful and quiet, and pausing to catch her breath. "It was very … very nice."

They were about a year out of high school. Jen was attending an area technical college to become a dental hygienist. Scott had stayed local and continued to work for a rain gutter company where he had worked part-time during high school. About nine months after graduation, Scott started working for a manufacturer of pressure treated lumber where they made products such as railroad ties and utility poles. Scott never worked a desk job. He always worked a lot of hours, always outside, always doing physical labor. He really enjoyed being a "hands-on" guy. "Even during the winter months, he never wanted to be cooped up inside," Jen remembered.

They were married at twenty-four and had their first daughter Kaylee at twenty-eight.

During those first years together, Scott and Jen worked hard to get ahead. After Kaylee was born they enjoyed camping on weekends with their little one nestled in a cradle in the corner of their tent. Jen said, "It was fun, because we didn't know any differently. Life was simple. We enjoyed each other's company while raising a baby, and Kaylee was such a good baby. We really relied on one another. We had a very good relationship together."

"Life was really good; and it was good because of family. My mother passed away before Kaylee was born. So, I didn't have my mom to help me," Jen remembered. "So, I relied on Scott's mother and family—a lot. But, Scott's family wasn't the talkative, robust family that I had grown up with. They were much more reserved than what I had experienced in my upbringing, which was totally opposite with much more hugging, kissing, dancing, and saying 'I love you' all the time. My family was somewhat loud and talkative. Scott came from a family which was more quiet and reserved."

At first Scott was a bit uncomfortable with his new family of in-laws. He didn't think he was going to fit in. Jen told me, "I brought out a lot in him. We were opposites. When I first started dating him, he didn't even want to go to a movie, he didn't want to go out to eat, and he didn't want to go out with my friends, because he was so reserved and quiet. He knew the type of person I was—outgoing and outspoken. In fact, I think he was kind of afraid that I was going to make him do things that he wasn't comfortable with."

As time went on, Scott became more comfortable talking about himself and his feelings, and about life. He even began to crack jokes, which was unusual for him. But, it was there, deep down inside. He just needed someone to help bring it to the surface, and that person was Jen.

"Our kids mirror us," Jen shared. "Kaylee is Scott, one hundred percent, and our daughter Madisyn is me, the social butterfly."

-----

Jen and Scott came to my office for a regular review of their life insurance policies and investments just a few months prior to Scott's diagnosis. Sometimes, even though someone owns a particular product, the details can be easily forgotten. During our visit we discussed conversion options, waiver of premium benefits, accelerated death benefit arrangements, ownership, and beneficiary designations. Oftentimes the belief many people have is that once you own a life insurance policy or have a completed will with an attorney, you can simply check off a box that says, "I don't have to review this again; thank goodness it's done." The opposite is true.

While in my office, they shared with me some small, but annoying physical difficulties Scott was beginning to experience. "The doctors had ruled out multiple sclerosis, seizures, strokes, and Lyme disease. They had ruled out so many things," Jen said.

As Scott walked ahead of us as they left my office that day, I remember leaning in close to Jen to ask, "Have the doctors checked Scott for ALS?" She said they had, and that they were ninety-five percent certain that he did not have Lou Gehrig's disease. Later on Jen would tell me that she didn't think the doctors wanted the answer to be ALS, and that she believed they wanted to eliminate all other possibilities first, before making that diagnosis.

Scott's health didn't get better. "In September," Jen recalls, "Scott began having muscle fasciculations or twitching over his entire body. Imagine having an eye twitch, but it's over your entire upper body and you can't stop them. It constantly goes and goes and goes. That was the hardest part for Scott to deal with right away, because it seemed like there was something underneath his skin constantly poking at him. Sometimes if he would put pressure on it, it would go away, but if he stopped applying pressure, it would return. Scott endured through this twenty-four hours a day, seven days a week."

Finally, they went to the Mayo Clinic in Rochester, Minn., to redo Scott's testing, all over again. It was December. The tests were inconclusive. They returned again the following August, and they did all the same tests—again. Scott had lost more mobility, and that's when his doctor said, "I think you're atypical for ALS."

"When it comes to achieving a diagnosis," Jen told me, "you simply rule out everything else first; and then, when you have Scott's symptoms remaining, you realize he has it."

Even with the passage of time, Jen looked at me with frustration as she remembered that day, saying "The doctor we had was an ass." She continued, "It was the doctor, Scott, Scott's mother, Carolyn, and me in that cold clinic room. After doing the initial testing of Scott's strength and looking at his tongue and then his pupils and having Scott walk some more, the doctor left and then returned to the examination room. We were all sitting there as the doctor sat at his computer. He then turned toward us and said, 'You're atypical for ALS.' Then he turned away from us and back to his computer to begin typing once more. Carolyn, Scott, and I were stunned. I said, 'Excuse me, what did you say?' There should have been a nurse or someone with more compassion in that room to show more sympathy for us."

"At that point, we didn't know what to do or where to turn; we had no answers and the doctor didn't offer any to us. So, I asked 'What do we do next?' The doctor said 'We will schedule some follow-up appointments, and I'll get you some information on where you may be able to begin looking for care.' He then gave us the name of a social worker and all the other departments we would be seeing during our follow-up visits. We felt alone".

Finally, Scott's mom asked, "Is there anything we can do to slow this down or is there anything we can do now in the meantime?" "No," was the reply. "This is something you just have to live with." Scott sat in silence as Jen and Carolyn tried to fish for any additional answers from the doctor.

-----

Today when asked, Jen believes that Scott already knew and had accepted that he had ALS, since all the other possibilities had been ruled out time and time again. "He knew," she said. "He told me quite a few times afterward, he knew".

Jen recalled asking the doctor how long Scott could be expected to live, tearing up as she relived that moment. They were told that most ALS patients live six months to five years. "When someone tells you that," Jen continued, "that is the hardest part, to hear those words. Finally, we asked if we could take a few moments to process what we had just been told and the doctor almost flippantly said, 'Take all the time you need.' He finished his notes, closed his computer program and left the room. He didn't even offer to have someone come to be with us; not a nurse or a social worker during a time when we really needed the support and more information on what to do next. We must have sat there for at least a half-hour, crying and talking and looking at one another and wondering, 'What do we do now?'"

When they returned home, Scott and Jen had a lot of heart-to-heart conversations, she remembers. "What do you want? Whatever you want, Scott," Jen told him. "I will do it for you, no matter what." His wishes were to remain at home and to work for as long as he could.

The changes to Scott's health seemed to come on gradually and with subtlety from then on. The disease began showing itself in Scott's right hand with the padding between his index finger and his thumb. Scott, who was right-handed, watched the muscle seemingly disappear as it sank into the palm of his hand; his hand began to curl into itself; and Scott lost function. The disease continued up his arm making it appear grey in color, where strong muscle had once been. Scott never lost feeling in any of his extremities though. "You could touch his fingers and his hands," Jen said. "There was never any numbness or tingling, but you could tell that the changes were going on."

Things didn't change overnight. It wasn't as if one day Scott was walking and the next day he wasn't. Instead, he was walking, and then his toes dropped, followed by occasional stumbling and then a couple of times Scott fell at home, frightening Jen. Once, Scott hit his head and knocked himself out in a fall to the floor. "We had just had a party at the house," said Jen. "My brother Terry lives about a mile away and volunteers as a township first-responder. So, I rolled Scott over and called my brother.

"Before Terry arrived, I was able to wake Scott and ask him some simple questions, like do you know who you are, do you know where you are, who am I, where do you live and how old are you; that sort of thing. He knew all of that, but he didn't know that he was sick. I asked, 'Do you know what happened? Do you know why you fell? He answered no, so I explained it to him.'"

"This part of the journey was hard to see," Jen continued, "with the beginning of the stumbling, you knew what that next step was going to be. After the loss of walking, you know what comes next."

-----

During this time, there were additional trips to my office. The next time I saw Scott, it was just a few months after our previous appointment. Now, Scott entered my office with the help of a motorized scooter, no longer trusting his legs. During this visit, we completed paperwork to initiate his policy's waiver of premium benefit. That would allow Scott's policy to be paid by the life insurance company, because of his disability. It would eliminate the responsibility of any future premium payments.

In addition, we worked together with Scott and Jen's attorney, Dan, who had assisted in completing their wills years earlier. It's not often that the opportunity of time is provided to any of us to thoroughly revisit these lasting legal documents prior to our death. Together they were able to receive counsel as to what they wanted life to be like after Scott's death, not only for Jen, but for Kaylee and Madisyn, too. I visited with Dan several times as we discussed ownership and beneficiary designations, trust options, potential trust investments and distribution arrangements that would take place after Scott's death.

Jen said that she felt that she "needed to prepare now for what was going to happen in three months, six months, a year, or three years down the road." She continued, "I wanted to go home the day of Scott's diagnosis at Mayo Clinic and complete as much paperwork, as I could; that's me! Scott would want to put a few things off, but I said to him, we just have to do this. Because what happens if you do pass in six months and things haven't been taken care? We took a lot of things out of Scott's name, because the state looks at all of your assets, of course. So, we needed to make sure he didn't have any. That was tough for him to take his name off of a lot of things he helped to build. The house was still in our name together though, but everything else was taken off. It's almost like a slap in the face, but reality is, I had to do this for me and the girls."

When it was time to apply for Social Security disability payments, Jen came into my office to begin the process. We sat together at a computer filling out the initial online application. We finished it by completing the final paragraph, which we wrote together for the remarks section, before submitting the form and receiving an eight-digit confirmation number.

It read: "I am physically only able to work eighteen hours per week. Due to the extreme work accommodations of my employer, exceptions have been made to continue my near-term employment. I use to do hard manual labor. But, my employer has allowed me to do simple deskwork, which I still find difficult. Any additional hours of compensation have been donated by my fellow employees for my benefit. I probably will not be able to continue working beyond a month or two."

Scott was able to continue working until October. Eventually, he lost so much strength in his hand that he couldn't even work a computer mouse in the office, after management had eased him inside from his regular outside job. During this transition, his company and coworkers were unbelievably wonderful. There were people who donated more than eighty hours of their personal time to give to Scott, so he could get a paycheck for almost four additional months. Every person donated time to Scott. His employer also gave Scott and the family a trip to Disney World. Scott had worked for Stella-Jones for twenty-one years and, through all those years, Jen told me she didn't think Scott had taken more than a total of five sick days.

Unfortunately, completing the online Social Security application, though it probably took a little over an hour, was actually the easy part. Later Jen remarked: "Social Security was awful. It was like talking to a brick wall with those people."

Continuing, Jen said "Thankfully, if there was anything that I didn't understand through this whole process, I would make sure I would either call someone to find out, or I would go to them myself, or look it up. I needed to know exactly what I was dealing with through everything. If I didn't understand something, I came to you, or I went to Dan, and I would say, 'I don't understand this, please explain this to me'."

This team approach helped to ensure the elimination of their mortgage and any remaining debt, it established a financial power of attorney and healthcare directives for

Scott, and it provided a trust for the family's support and the girls' education.

-----

Scott and Jen had been married for sixteen years when they received the diagnosis of ALS. I had met them about thirteen years earlier when Scott was twenty-seven. Now, at the age of forty, they were entering an unknown future. Kaylee was twelve, and Maddy was seven.

"When Scott was diagnosed," Jen told me later, "we had a talk within the first few weeks with the girls. 'This is what Dad has. This is what is going to happen. Do you have any questions?' And at that time, neither one of them had any."

But, as the months went on, the family would sit down about once per month at the dinner table and talk about the changes going on with Scott. They talked about when he started to loose strength in his right hand, when his toes started to drop, and how that meant he was beginning to walk differently. Jen says they would ask the girls each time: "Is there anything you girls would like to know? You each have to ask at least one question. We don't care what it is."

This forced them to think about what was happening. The questions that were asked and answered:
"Is Dad still going to be able to go to work?" "Yes, for a short period of time."
"Is Dad still going to be able to walk?" "Yes, for a short period of time."

"So, we tried to share and explain to them whenever Scott would have a major change in his condition," Jen said.

Leading up to Scott's death, Madisyn was very strong, actively helping Jen with the day-to-day tasks of Scott's care. "There was nothing she would not do," Jen shared. "Kaylee broke down more and wore her heart on her sleeve and took it the hardest. Don't get me wrong, Madisyn did her fair share of crying. But, Kaylee would ask more often, why is this happening? Why?"

"I wish we would have had better treatment earlier," Jen repeated.

Scott's diagnosis in August was his last appointment with the physician who had left them feeling so alone. After that visit, a new doctor who had just arrived from the northwestern United States took over Scott's treatment. He specialized in neurological diseases. Scott was one of his first patients and from that point on, he was seeing him about every four to six weeks.

"During the last year, I was a total caregiver," Jen continued. "Scott could not do anything for himself. He couldn't feed himself. He had an upper G.I. tube placed through his stomach to eat in addition to a catheter; it was because, after Scott would eat certain foods, I was in fear of him choking, because his tongue no longer worked. Since your tongue is a muscle, it no longer functions correctly; and you're not able to put food where it needs to be, so you can't chew it to the consistency to swallow."

"Early on, Scott said he didn't want a feeding tube to eat or a tracheotomy to breath. He did not want either one," Jen said. For months, they talked about it everyday, and Scott continued not wanting to have a tracheotomy, because he did not want to be placed on a ventilator. But, to live another year, he chose to have a feeding tube.

"Both of our girls were very helpful with Scott's feeding," Jen recalls. "The liquid is hooked up to what looks similar to an I.V. bag and it goes right into the stomach taking about forty-five minutes to an hour to empty; and that was done three times per day, sometimes four. Because of the feeding tube, it was difficult to plan our days. Over this time Scott's weight went from two hundred-twenty pounds to a little over one-seventy on his six foot, four inch frame, when he passed."

During the time of Scott's sickness, Jen also needed to take care of herself, so she wouldn't be injured, as she needed to move Scott from one place to another. She would work out every morning, five days per week. Scott's mom and sister would come over while he was still sleeping. That was Jen's time to get out of the house. It was time for herself, yet she was doing it for him by keeping her strength and personal wellbeing up, to benefit him; plus it was also respite care for Jen for that hour or two while she was away. Scott needed someone there 24/7; he could not be left alone for any reason, whatsoever.

Communication became more difficult, as time went on. Scott used a machine to speak. Early on, he could use his hand to click the letters or the words he wanted to communicate. The machine also had phrases like "Scratch my ear" or "hello, my name is Scott. I have ALS." Then after he could no longer use his hands, he needed to only look at a specific square and the word or phrase would go to the top of the screen and then it would be repeated verbally for those around him to hear. But it was slow and time-consuming. For Scott to say "scratch my ear" through the computer took nearly a minute. The machine could also change the channel on the TV and turn the lights of the room on and off. These were the few things in his life he could still control.

"We could see the frustration in his face," Jen said, "and it was frustrating for us to try and understand him, as well. There were times when he tried to speak a few words and it was frustrating to say 'I can't understand what you're saying'."

Scott didn't smile a lot towards the end. He tried, but it wasn't his normal smile. Yet, it is one thing a lot of people commented about. Scott never lost his will to smile through the whole thing. But, you could see the fatigue in his eyes, you could see the stress he was under, the weariness and confusion of what he was going through; and the desire to have those around him understand, but they couldn't. So, for the most part, he watched a lot of television. He listened to a lot of music. He would listen to the Bible. His mother would read to him. But, the inability to speak was the hardest part. Scott continued to try and speak up until the last few weeks.

I asked Jen during a visit later, "Did Scott ever get mad?" "Yes," she replied. "But it was probably more frustration than anger. Getting mad wasn't going to solve anything. So, at least by getting frustrated, I could try and fix it or try and make it better. Hospice was there three times each week. They gave him baths in bed, because after six months of doing it myself, I wasn't able to any longer. I wasn't strong enough to roll him over. I needed someone to help me."

"It was a lot of work. In addition of the catheter, I had to take care of the rest of the toileting, too; and I got pretty darn good at that," Jen continued. "At this point in my life nothing fazes me or grosses me out, because when you need to take care of a loved one, such as a parent or a spouse or a child, there just isn't anything that fazes me anymore. I have grown up so much. 'Let it go' is a phrase I have used a lot. Deal with it and move on. I've seen my life as hurdles in a race. Everything we went through with Scott was a hurdle. Every step along the way, when you need help, you find someone to help you over that next hurdle. I was never one to ask for help and neither was Scott. Both of us were very independent and didn't want to have to rely on others.

"But, it got to where I could ask for help from anyone, because I knew there are so many people who were willing to help. When it came time that we really needed the help, so many people were there for us."

The journey of Scott's final week began on a Sunday morning while Jen was getting ready for church. Scott wasn't going. "I was getting myself and the girls ready", Jen recalled. "Scott had a nosebleed. His mom was going to come over to the house. So, I was cleaning him up and washed his face. After momentarily leaving the room, I returned and the nosebleed had started again. I applied some pressure and sat him up a little bit. At that point we also had a suction unit in the room to take care of any mucus Scott would have. The nosebleed continued to get worse and worse and worse. It was getting pretty bad. I told Maddy to call grandma and have her come over. I needed some help.

"Before Carolyn got to the house, the blood had probably gone down his throat and into his stomach. Before she arrived, Scott threw up. I had aspirated a lot of the mucus and blood, but it wasn't enough to keep some of it from going down into his lungs and causing pneumonia".

Scott woke up in the middle of that Sunday night and communicated that he thought Jen should call their pastor. So, she called thinking that this might be the end.

By Monday though, Scott was actually feeling a little bit better. "I could tell by his breathing. He still had between fifty to sixty percent air capacity in his lungs, which was good. By then the hospice nurse came every day; and on Tuesday morning, Scott told the girls that he loved them and to have a great day at school and he would see them when they got home."

By that evening, he closed his eyes and became comatose. "He had told me and his parents that he was ready, that he loved us, and he said 'Whenever God takes me home, I am ready.'" Jen said. He had said that a lot during the last few months. By Tuesday evening, Scott's eyes closed for the last time.

Kaylee's birthday was Thursday. Scott passed away on Friday, at 7:30 in the morning. His father had just gotten there that morning. Someone was with Scott the entire time towards the end in the event he needed to be aspirated. Scott's mom had just left to go home to shower after spending the night with Scott. At one point on Wednesday, a nurse had said she would be surprised if he would live through the night. Scott lasted two more days.

"I don't think he wanted to pass on Kaylee's birthday. So, he resisted the end, one more day," Jen said.

-----

"We had so many people to our home, probably over a hundred as they came into our bedroom, from that Sunday until the Friday when he died. People came and sang. They played guitar. They read scripture. They brought gifts. They brought food for the family. They came. We held hands. We prayed together with Scott. We talked about good times. We talked about high school. We talked about camping. We talked about everything. You know, every time someone would come in, I would say, talk to Scott, as if his eyes were wide-open, because he can hear you."

Very softly, Jen looked at me with her eyes filling with tears and with a low soft voice said, "That whole last week, I did not cry." She paused and wiped a tear from the corner of her eye with her right hand and repeated, "I did not cry." "And I tell you," she continued, with her voice becoming a mere whisper, "I think I was so relieved when Scott actually passed."

"For him?" I asked. "Yea," Jen confirmed. "I just ... I broke down that morning. I didn't cry again for another week, until the church service, because I think I was so exhausted. I slept so little during the last week of Scott's life, because I wanted to be awake when he passed."

-----

"I was sitting at the dining room table as Scott's father had just walked behind me and had just gone into the bedroom to sit down with Scott," Jen describes that last morning. "His mom had just come out and was going home to shower. I sat down at the dining room table and had a pen in my hand. I had my checkbook out to pay bills. That's what I was doing. Gerald came out of the room and said, 'He's gone.' I put my things down, got up from the chair, went to the bedroom, sat down beside him and held his hand."

"We had talked and planned for this day. There wasn't anything to do; it was already set in motion," Jen said. "We had music picked out; the obituary had been written; all the paperwork that people put off for months, and months, and months. People just don't do it. But, we had already completed everything. When people die in an automobile accident and are here today and gone tomorrow, there's little time. Instead, we had the time to ask Scott, what do you want? Tell me. So, I don't have to guess later on".

Regarding the life insurance, all Jen had to do was bring me the death certificate and sign a form. That's all.

"I believe our two girls will appreciate everything so much more in their lives, Madisyn, perhaps even more then Kaylee, even though she's younger, just because she was so helpful and hands on. The only thing Madisyn did not do was to help me when Scott went to the bathroom. Everything else, she was there. She was right next to me when Scott had that nosebleed during his last week, handing me towels and suctioning and wiping his face. She never cried nor questioned, but would simply say, 'What do you need now, Mom?' 'What can I help you with, Mom?'"

-----

## Chapter Nineteen

Toward the end of our visit together gathering their story for this book, I asked Jen "What do you wish you knew then, that you know now or that you learned along this journey?"

"I wish I would have had more patience," was her reply, "patience for all of Scott's needs. What I did for Scott was everything I could have done. I don't think I could have done anything more or better for him. Quitting my job to care for him was probably the most difficult thing for me to do, because I really enjoyed it."

That really says something about the Jen I know. Some spouses facing the reality of an illness of this magnitude would have elected to seek out a facility for Scott's end-of-life care. But, that wasn't what Scott wanted. He wanted to be at home. Jen understood the need and the responsibility for Scott's continued care at home.

"The way in which Scott and I prepared financially, our girls should be able to follow whatever ambitions and dreams they have for their future," Jen said. "I don't have to be concerned. They're going to be okay. I can provide for myself. But, Scott's life insurance will help me to provide for them. They're being taken care of. All the options are there for our girls' future and I don't have to worry about it … I can't thank you enough, Mark."

"Scott wanted me to be happy," Jen said, choking up as we discussed Scott's journey together. "This is probably the most that I've broken down in six months. I don't cry, and,"—she paused—"I think that, that's a good thing. Scott is watching down on us. I don't believe he's upset.

He's running. He's dancing. He's laughing. He's talking. One of the things Scott wanted to put in his obituary, instead of saying 'rest in peace,' he wanted it to say that he was 'Running in peace.' He didn't want to rest, he wanted to run."

-----

As I reflect on my time serving Scott and Jen's family, I realize that even at a young age, Scott and Jen planned the details of their life, instead of "making it up" as they went along. They listened to the advice of Jen's father to prepare as they established their journey together. Most couples may not even consider life insurance prior to the birth of their first child. Instead, Scott and Jen saw it as a prerequisite along with meeting with an attorney to prepare a will. All of this was the first part of beginning a family together.

Though the premiums for their life insurance were a stretch for their modest budget, they realized their future potential earnings needed to be protected in the event of an early death. In addition, acquiring a life insurance policy with a waiver of premium benefit that would pay the premiums in the event of a disability, eliminated payments to free up money to be used for their new expenses—like a ramp to enter their home from the garage or handicap bars in the bathroom shower.

Having the extra time also allowed Scott and Jen to receive additional counsel as to the ownership and beneficiary designations of their life insurance policies to allow for proper estate and trust planning. During times of a lengthy illness that may end in death, it's almost like being given a "do-over" opportunity. Unfortunately, no do-overs are allowed when you want to purchase additional life insurance. Life insurance is paid for with money, but it's bought with your health, and Scott bought his life insurance when he was young and healthy. It can't be purchased when you need it. Then, it's too late. You have to "want it" and want it today!

But, since they owned life insurance that could not be taken away from them, they had a tool that no investment could have replicated. Also, the tax-free death benefit allowed the full value to be used to continue the family's life without a husband and father, debt-free, along with a stream of income for now and a trust account for later needs, such as education for the girls.

November is a good time to remember Scott's life and the decision he and Jen made for each other and their family. It's a reason for Thanksgiving.

-----

As I sipped my morning coffee at the kitchen table on the Monday following Scott's death, I read the daily newspaper and quietly acknowledged Scott's passing, pausing as I slowly read his obituary. I noticed a name I did not recognize, at the very end of the list of those who had preceded Scott in death. It simply said – "and one special friend, Melissa." Who was she?

As Scott traversed his journey with ALS, Missy—a dear friend of his—was voyaging through the unknown territory of breast cancer that she knew would eventually take her life, just as ALS would take Scott's. While Scott and Jen had two girls, Missy and her husband, James, had three boys. They had been experiencing many of the same worries about their future while trying to navigate their present life.

As close friends, these two couples found themselves supporting one another, as only they knew how. Jen would share that she didn't know what Scott and Missy talked about during their private times together, but it might have centered around their fear of dying, perhaps the fear of the unknown, maybe the fear of losing control of their own destinies. It likely also included sharing their strong faith in God and what his will would be for the remainder of their lives and for their families after their own deaths.

As Missy and Scott visited, Jen and James would find themselves discussing many of the same concerns, but from the vantage point of caregivers for their spouses now and wondering what life would be like without them, later.

Missy died at the age of thirty-seven. On the day of her death that summer, Jen, Scott, and the girls were on the way home from a birthday party. James called Jen's cell phone. As she drove and listened, she repeated to Scott and the girls of Missy's passing. The look on Scott's face was as if he was socked in the stomach. He lost the one and only friend who understood the intimate end-of-life journey he, himself, was on. The van was quiet the rest of the drive home. It probably felt especially upsetting to Scott, since because of his immobility, he couldn't personally say goodbye to Missy during her last days.

After Missy's death, James purposely did not reach out for help. Some even criticized him for that. He felt a need to prove to himself that he could overcome and succeed by doing it on his own. James probably didn't think of that at the time but looking back at it now, he thought to himself, "If I can get through this now, a really hard place; then later on, if I ask for help, it would only become easier."

While James forged on without Missy, he didn't forget his friends, Scott and Jen, who were still traveling an uncertain road to its final known conclusion. He would sometimes send a text to Jen during the day, asking if there was anything she needed, any way he could help? Could he take the girls for a couple of hours or did Jen need to get out of the house for a while? Could he come over and sit with Scott?

Jen said, "He just reached out to me and kind of put a note in the back of my mind," saying to herself, that this is a very good man. "I knew what he had gone through losing Missy," she would later say. At one point Scott sent James an email that said in part, "I love you like a brother that I never had." James would be one of Scott's pallbearers when it came time for his funeral.

After Scott's passing, James remembered thinking to himself, "I know how I felt when Missy passed. It was awful and I'm not going to let my friend (Jen) go through that alone."

As Scott was progressively debilitated by the disease taking hold of his body, Jen became less of a spouse and more of a caregiver. Her love never failed, but her role changed, as she helped Scott through his journey. After Scott's death, James and Jen began to feel that perhaps there was a stronger connection between them, more than just close friends.

While caring for their spouses, Jen and James also found themselves talking for hours trying to provide support for one another. So, when they decided to date, they soon realized that they probably knew each other better within the first six months of dating than many people did after six years of marriage. They knew each other's backgrounds; each other's emotions, feelings, anxieties, and dreams; and the values each wanted to instill in their children. They were truly on the same page since they had each been exposed to the book of each other's lives.

Some people thought it was too soon: they were dating too soon, they got engaged too soon. But, they hadn't just met. Their love evolved together over the time that their lives had intertwined through the passage their spouses had endured, spouses that they each dearly loved and missed.

When they realized that the trajectory of their love meant marrying and combining their families, they wanted the blessings of their children.

"The one for whom it was probably the most difficult was Kaylee," Jen said. "She said 'Mom, I think it's too soon for you.'"

Jen paused and pondered, "I wondered, is it because she's fourteen and she just lost her dad. But after James and I talked with her and explained that this is what her Dad would have wanted for me; not to be alone for the rest of my life; and who more to spend the rest of my life with, than someone I wasn't going to have to search for. He is right here! And I told her, 'James loves you guys as much as he loves his own three children'."

They were married in September, a little less than a year after Scott's death.

James interjected during our visit, "After going through the previous three to four years, Jen and I realize that life is short. Anything can happen to anyone on any given day. And to know that this is the person for me—why would I wait?"

Investments Don't Hug

# Chapter Twenty

*The Default Worst Case Scenario*

I called a friend of mine recently who happens to be the president of a local bank with a question regarding mortgage loans. "Suppose," I began, "that I had a thirty-year home mortgage at a bank and let's suppose that I had just made my three hundred and fifty-ninth monthly payment, and let's suppose that I didn't make my very last payment—number three hundred and sixty. Due to circumstances beyond my control, I had no money and no way of getting any money from anywhere to pay my very last mortgage payment. What would happen?" I asked. "There's no money, at all?" he questioned. "Nothing," I replied. "Let's pretend I didn't have a job. I didn't have any savings and I didn't have any friends or family. Let's pretend, that other than my house, I am completely broke. What then?"

My banker friend paused and said, "As a bank, we would try to work with that person and get that last payment. Plus, we can't just foreclose on a person's house and take possession the very next month. The bank would have to take a year or more to work out a plan or to initiate a foreclosure of the property."

"So, there aren't any stipulations written into a mortgage agreement guaranteeing the homeowner predetermined options regarding the equity in their home in the event of a default of their mortgage loan, even if it's the very last payment?" I asked. "No," was his reply.

As I shared this story with a local attorney, he commented that when a mortgage foreclosure occurs in the event of a mortgage not being paid, the bank has the right to have the house sold. The bank gets the amount owed, and the balance of the sale proceeds would go to the homeowner. An extreme example with a different outcome could be that of a "land contract" with an option of a strict foreclosure, he told me. If you were to buy a property under a land contract and you didn't make that last payment, the person acting as "the bank" could file a strict foreclosure that would force the property back, and you might forfeit all the payments you had made.

To try and obtain a more favorable outcome could require the homeowner taking this case to court to seek a more equitable approach, more in line with standard statutory foreclosure rules. But here's the thing, now we're talking attorneys, courts, and an unknown amount of time. As we saw during the real estate mortgage crisis at the height of The Great Recession, those resolutions were drawn out for some homeowners for years.

-----

At some point in the discussion of whole life insurance policies, the question is sometimes asked, when can I stop paying the premium or what happens if I stop paying the premium on this life insurance policy? This is a question that would rarely be asked about mortgage loans, automobile loans, or personal loans, since the responsible thing to do is to keep paying and building equity or paying off debt. But, we also understand, as pointed out by the conversation with my banker and attorney friends, that my home could be foreclosed on, my car could be repossessed, or any other items could be taken from me, if held as collateral, even if I had a substantial amount of value contained in any one of those assets.

Continuing with the home/whole life insurance analogy we used earlier, let's think of a whole life insurance policy as similar to a long-term mortgage with a set payment amount, a set initial value, and a set level of equity being accrued each month. But, unlike our home mortgage example, which doesn't provide any contractual safeguards when payments stop, a whole life insurance policy does. These safeguards are called "non-forfeiture provisions," and they're written into each whole life insurance contract. They're generally found near the end of a policy.

The first non-forfeiture option is the easiest to understand. It's called "cash." The day you cancel a life insurance policy should be considered one of the saddest days of your life, because you are giving up an asset that is now virtually irreplaceable. In all likelihood, you will never be as healthy as the day you initially purchased your original policy and most definitely you would never be the same age again as when you first acquired that policy. The winner here is not you. In my opinion, it's the insurance company.

For all these years, you've been paying premiums to build up this permanent asset. In fact, with each passing year, the chance of the life insurance policy actually paying a death benefit has increased! Yet, there are some people who no longer believe that they need the coverage when they're older. When I pay off my thirty-year mortgage, do I cancel my homeowner's insurance? When I pay off my automobile loan, do I cancel my car insurance? No!

The state you live in might require you to have an insurance policy if you drive a car, but I have never seen a law that requires you to have a homeowner's insurance policy (other than the bank requiring you to have a policy if you owe them money on your home through a mortgage loan—because, of course, they want "their asset" to be protected).

Isn't it silly then for you to cancel a life insurance policy at the very time that the odds of your death are ratcheting up each year? Individuals who own term life insurance begin seeing their future premiums rising along with their rising chance of death. Remember, standard whole life insurance policies typically have a fixed premium for the life of the contract. Since whole life insurance can provide certainty, if you needed money, wouldn't it make more sense to spend down your other assets first, allowing the insurance money to be used for your safe money and then leaving that money, which may very well end up becoming the last money left "on the table" when you and your estate come to an end. It's my opinion that this is the best last asset.

Why should a life insurance policy be called an asset? You don't need to go any further than a life insurance company's own financial balance sheet. When you own a life insurance policy, the net amount of risk the insurance company has taken on with the issuance of your policy is called a liability. Because of this liability, the insurance company is required to hold onto a certain level of reserves, which is a requirement of your state's department of insurance.

Think back to an asset/liability statement that you might have seen in a high school or college accounting class. These statements list assets on one side of the balance sheet and liabilities on the opposite side. When the numbers are totaled at the bottom, the assets should equal the liabilities. So, if the "risk" of your life insurance policy is listed as a liability of the insurance company, whose asset is it? It's your asset! Furthermore, if you cancel your life insurance policy, who has now eliminated a liability? The insurance company.

If the insurance company has eliminated a liability, using the balance sheet example, someone has now lost an asset. Who might that be? The answer is that you have lost an asset.

Let's say you own a $1,000,000 whole life insurance policy with a cash surrender value of $250,000, leaving the insurance company with $750,000 of "risk" or liability on their books. If you cancel your policy, you have released the insurance company of their $750,000 responsibility. You got $250,000 in your pocket. But, you also have lost a permanent asset. The winner here might actually be the life insurance company who just reduced a huge liability. Why do I get a strange feeling that they're having a party in your honor at the home office at the end of the week with a big cake, because you just cancelled your policy? You paid premiums all those years and now that you're older and closer to your eventual demise, you're letting the insurance company off the hook?! What sense does that make?

-----

So, the first non-forfeiture provision in a life insurance policy is usually "cash" which you would receive by surrendering your whole life insurance policy for its net surrender value. The amount you would receive may be reduced by any outstanding policy loans that you might have taken out previously against your policy.

The second non-forfeiture provision we'll discuss is "reduced paid-up insurance." Let's use the premium-paying $1,000,000 whole life insurance policy example mentioned above, with a surrender value of $250,000 once more.

Using our house example, let's say you have been paying monthly payments on a $1,000,000 house that has an equity balance of $250,000. One day you decide that you no longer wish to make any more house payments. In addition, you are comfortable with the idea of downsizing, since you still need a place to live. With some variations depending upon whether you're a man or a woman and how old you are when you elect to take advantage of this option, you can accomplish the exact same concept with a whole life insurance policy. In fact, the "exchange" or non-forfeiture values have already been predetermined contractually inside your policy. Here's what it might look like.

Instead of living in a $1,000,000 house which requires a monthly mortgage payment, you simply exchange it for a $500,000 house with no mortgage payment with the equity you built up in your the first house. That's a reduced paid-up whole life insurance policy!

The actual values depend on your own specific situation, but the concept is the same. No more premium payments, but a reduced amount of life insurance coverage. At this point, you may wonder why the insurance amount is greater than the "equity" or cash surrender portion of the life insurance policy, when in a house example the equity and the price of the paid-up house is the same. Remember, to be classified as life insurance, there always needs to be an insured amount in excess of the cash value of the policy, until the policy matures or endows, typically at the age of 121.

An important stipulation to note is that once a whole life insurance policy has used the non-forfeiture option to become a reduced paid-up policy, this option cannot be reversed. The amount of life insurance coverage cannot be increased and no further premium payments are allowed, even if you wished to put more money into it. One important feature that remains, with the new paid-up life insurance policy is that it will have its own schedule of guaranteed cash value increases each year, and the policy will also be eligible for dividends as the company may declare them annually. If the dividends are used to purchase additional paid-up insurance, not only will the internal cash values increase, but so will the "external" death benefit.

A third non-forfeiture option available with a whole life insurance policy is called "extended term insurance." Personally, I have never used this option in my practice. The appropriate situation hasn't presented itself, but it's an option nonetheless.

Let's return to our $1,000,000 house example once more. Remember, we also have an equity or cash value of $250,000. Let's pretend that you love your house and you don't want to downsize. You also don't wish to or can't make the mortgage payments any longer. Wouldn't it be clever if your mortgage contract allowed you to use the equity inside your home as rent payments so you wouldn't have to make any further monthly payments out-of-pocket, allowing you to remain in your house for a predetermined period of time? That's exactly how extended term insurance works.

Remember, I am simply making these "example" numbers up, so you understand the concept of how extended term insurance works. Each individual contract will be unique to the specific insured. Are you forty years old or seventy-five? Are you male or female? Do you smoke or are you a non-smoker? Have you owned your policy for ten years or have you had it for twenty years? A whole life insurance policy and its non-forfeiture options are specifically calculated for the specific person with very specific and exact numbers at specific intervals.

Here's how the concept of extended term insurance works in its general form. You no longer wish to pay the premium on your whole life insurance policy. Easy enough, those premiums end.

You still want $1,000,000 of life insurance coverage. Easy enough; based on the $250,000 of "equity" or cash value in our example, that insurance coverage can continue.

The third element though, is how long will this coverage last? That timeframe is based on the dollar amounts and the specifics mentioned earlier. Again, I'm simply making these numbers up so you can conceptualize how this works.

Your $1,000,000 of life insurance coverage may last for the next twenty-three years and one hundred fourteen days. Yes, the calculation is actually that precise, and that's why it's different for each individual. In this example, that's how long the insurance coverage may last. If you were to die just one day after that expiration date, there would be no death benefit paid, just like any other term life insurance policy. But, if you were to die before the expiration of the extended term insurance coverage, your beneficiaries would receive the death benefit and any unused premium.

-----

A whole life policy will typically include a page near the back of the insurance contract that will list the non-forfeiture values we've discussed. It will be arranged with vertical columns listing the following:

- Policy Year
- Age of the Insured, in that policy year
- Guaranteed Cash Value
- Paid-Up Insurance
- Extended Term Insurance, in Years and Days

Normally the first year through the twentieth year is listed. In addition, the values of when the insured reaches the age of fifty-five, sixty and sixty-five are usually listed as well. Upon request, the insurance company will also provide the calculations for other years.

All the values listed are based on the guaranteed values only, less any policy loans. Once a dividend is paid and added to your policy's cash values, all the future non-forfeiture options would become higher, as well.

There is one additional provision that should be discussed. It's not a non-forfeiture option, but it is a guarantee that is included inside a whole life insurance policy that many clients and their agents overlook. It's called a "Settlement Option Table." Usually, when death proceeds are paid to a beneficiary they are received in the form of a check or an account which the beneficiary can write checks against, as needed. While a check or an open-ended account are the mostly commonly used means of settling the policy, this section outlines additional options for the insured or for the beneficiaries.

The Settlement Option Table is usually a single page near the back of a whole life insurance policy. It includes multiple columns of numbers, based on the guarantees of the contract (assuming no dividends or outstanding loans against the policy).

In its simplest usage, think of this page as a summary of calculations to be used in creating a pension, whether you're a beneficiary receiving a death benefit or if you're the owner of the life insurance policy wishing to convert your contract into an income stream.

An "interest only" option could pay you a monthly, quarterly, semi-annual or annual payment of interest, leaving the balance of the money on deposit with the insurance company.

A "specific period" option would calculate how much income you could receive monthly, quarterly, semi-annually, or annually, based on the initial amount of money for a specific period of time, say ten or twenty years.

A "specific amount" option calculates how long (in years) your money would last, based on a specific dollar amount you would want to receive monthly, quarterly, semi-annually, or annually.

A "joint and survivor" option is similar to a standard pension, typically paying you for as long as you live and then a spouse, after your death, for as long as your spouse lives.

And a "lifetime" income option, most often used by a single individual. On several occasions, where a divorce has occurred later in life, I have assisted those clients who were interested in receiving a guaranteed income on a regular basis for the rest of their lives from their life insurance policy using this option.

In addition to these guaranteed non-forfeiture options of a whole life insurance policy, if a policy has received dividends throughout the years and if they have been left with the policy, those accumulated dividends may be used to pay your policy's premium, potentially allowing your policy to be maintained with little or no out-of-pocket cost without using any of the non-forfeiture provisions described previously.

It is seldom that any of the options discussed in this chapter are used, but it's important to understand the complex nature of some of the built-in tools that are available to you by owning a whole life insurance policy. Not only is this kind of policy constructed to last your whole life, but it's also agile enough to change and adapt, as you live your whole life.

# Conclusion

Jenny never knew it, but when she pointed her finger at me on that cold December day and said, "I'm not going to be one of your stories," the book you've just read began. Several years later, I visited with Jenny's husband, Brian, about his life since her death. As hard as the lesson is, life goes on; it has to.

Life insurance didn't change the outcome of Jenny's death. What it did provide was the elimination of financial concerns for the family. Brian, instead, could focus on raising their two young children in a world that was forever changed by Jenny's death.

Unexpected blessings frequently revealed themselves during the conversations I have with families in the years after their loved one's death. I have come to realize that investments play an ongoing role in the continuation of a family's financial wealth, no matter the size. But, investments do not necessarily provide the opportunity to offer the fullest potential to instill the continuing wealth of values that a family may wish to see take hold in the future of their family tree.

I've seen it played out, first hand. Life insurance has provided immediate debt elimination of mortgages, personal and business loans, as well as the normal estate expenses when a person dies.

Life insurance has provided moms and dads with the opportunity to scale back from work responsibilities allowing them to instead focus on family responsibilities, where they find themselves having to do the job of two parents.

Life insurance has given clients the opportunity to spend more of their hard earned money in retirement, by insuring their human life value, as an asset and as a leverage tool that can replace money spent during their retirement years, recreating it through the death benefit and passing it on to their families for a lasting impact for future generations.

I have seen life insurance used as a creative estate planning tool to specifically earmark wealth outside of the publicity of wills and the probate process to provide a private bequest.

Life insurance has offered dignity to clients when other resources were not available during the last months of life, providing access to the living benefits of a death benefit, without having to die first.

I have witnessed life insurance financing opportunities for greater potential gains than other options that might not be available through regular lenders or to liquidate other assets to acquire personal fulfillment and business gain.

Life insurance can shield your life's potential, by supplying financial backing for personal or business opportunities. It can help leverage your other financial assets to work more efficiently together as one cohesive financial strategy, as opposed to being limited by the single features of other individual financial products. It can also continue on its own, if you're disabled and unable to work. Yet, its greatest asset may be the peace of mind it provides. You can begin each day knowing that you're not in it all alone. Life insurance has your back.

The stories I've shared are just a handful that I have journeyed through with clients over my career. Some other narratives were too painful for me to recall in detail. None of us wish to admit the inevitable, because that future seems far off, down the road. We fool ourselves into believing, not me, not us, not now.

Those of faith realize that we are all specifically called upon to provide for our own, especially those in our own house, our own family (1Timothy 5:8). Life insurance is a way to guarantee that we fulfill that responsibility.

Frequently, clients may wish to refer family and friends to our office. When that conversation arises, I ask clients to reflect on their potential referral first. "When you have your next conversation with this person," I begin, "before you tell them anything about me, I would like you to press your 'pause button' and think about these two important values. Number one, ask yourself, 'Does this person love someone?'"

I'll usually receive a blank stare.

"Love someone?" will be the look returned from their faces. "Yes, do they love someone—a spouse, a child or a grandchild? Do they love someone? Puppies don't count," I'll continue, which inevitably solicits a laugh or a chuckle. "Because everyone loves puppies! But, do they love *someone?*"

There has to be love.

Secondly, I'll ask them to consider this question: "Does the person you're considering referring believe in a higher purpose, a higher calling? Do they believe that there is a reason we're all here as opposed to just spending our life on earth sucking air, in and out? If the person you would like to refer to me loves someone and believes in a greater good, a higher purpose, then disengage your 'pause button' and tell them about me."

The reason I have clients go through this exercise with all potential referrals they may wish to send to our office is that I simply can't and won't work with those that don't hold those two values.

Occasionally, someone will sneak through our prescreening process, because they might have found our office through a website or another source. What becomes frustrating is when a potential client arrives for an introductory meeting, and my gut tells me within the first several minutes of meeting them, that they don't embrace these two values. Sometimes, it's the body language of the person or the couple. Maybe it's the words they choose, but the wisdom of time has proven to me that it's got to be the right fit from the beginning, and sometimes from the very beginning I know it's not. I can't change another person's values. We have to be on the same page from the start. If not, it'll be a bad experience for both of us, and I want it to be a great experience for each of us.

The math of life insurance works. The value it can create as a living asset works. The value it can create as a death benefit works. To explain any specific concept for the uses of life insurance, through the use of math is relatively easy. But, if there's no love and no ultimate purpose as to why we are here in the first place, it almost always becomes a game of cutting corners, making due, getting by, and trying to do more for less. I wouldn't want to buy a house from a contractor who had that attitude as their construction plan. Similarly, I hope you wouldn't want your financial life to be built upon that same premise, either.

We've come full circle with Jenny's story from the introduction of this book. While discussing this manuscript with Jenny's husband, Brian, he looked at me with the same focused eyes that Jenny used while speaking to me years earlier. But, this time the words were different, as he understood in a too-personal way the important message of this book. Brian simply said, "You need to finish it."

Jenny and Brian, thank you for your initial inspiration and for your persistence in helping communicate that "investments don't hug" and that as part of a carefully planned financial strategy for ourselves and for our family, we all need to "embrace the life insurance asset."

What's next? I've discussed what to look for in an advisor and/or life insurance agent. You now have the basic understanding of how life insurance works and what it can do.

The next step is yours.

## About the author

Mark Bertrang was raised in Le Sueur, Minn.—a small rural community with a little more than 3,000 residents, nestled in a quiet river valley surrounded by acres of black fertile farmland. In his youth, kids were expected to work hard, respect their folks, and go to church on Sunday morning.

Though the community was close knit, it was separated by the jobs people held. Executives hired by the town's major employer worked "above the hill" on the Green Giant® company campus. Blue-collar workers labored "below the hill" near the company's vegetable canning factory. His family was proud to be "below the hill" people.

After attending school to enter the broadcasting field, Mark worked for a small family-owned radio station in Fairmont, Minn. After marrying his wife, Betty, they moved to Winona, Minn., and finally to Onalaska, a neighboring community of La Crosse, Wis., during which time he entered the financial services industry.

He earned his CLU® (Chartered Life Underwriter) designation in 1993 and his ChFC® (Chartered Financial Consultant) designation in 1995 from The American College in Bryn Mawr, Penn.

Through his career, Mark has enjoyed addressing his peers at conferences and association gatherings, sharing his passion for exceptional client service. At the heart of each presentation is a story. He has been a member of the Society of Financial Service Professionals since 1992. Mark acted as secretary/treasurer of the La Crosse, Wis., chapter for fifteen years. In addition, he served a term as president of the Mutual Trust General Agents' Association, in Oak Brook, Ill.

Prior to writing "Investments Don't Hug," his work has been published in industry and insurance company trade journals, and he has also shared his views on local-affiliated ABC, NBC, and FOX television news programs, in addition to regional newspapers.

Bertrang trademarked his process of working with clients, "The Financialoscopy®" in 2009.

Over the years, his free time has been centered on leadership within his church's youth program, including ten summer service trips to disadvantaged areas around the country. Mark has completed coursework to serve through his church as a Stephen Minister, trained to provide distinctive one-to-one Christian care to people going through tough times. He now serves his church as a lay leader.

A special concern to Mark is the misunderstanding of mental illness and how it silently affects the lives of families. He has participated in the National Association of Mental Illness "family–to–family" education program and has incorporated its message into his practice when dealing with families who have children with special needs.

## About the Author

In his free time, Mark enjoys escaping to a family cabin in the woods of northern Wisconsin, spending time relaxing along the Flambeau River.

For additional information, please visit his company website: financialoscopy.com

Made in the USA
Lexington, KY
14 August 2018